MW01689725

Thomas Gustave Plant

His Life and Legacy

Martha S. Grover

Marty Grover
Studio

THOMAS GUSTAVE PLANT

HIS LIFE AND LEGACY

THOMAS GUSTAVE PLANT

HIS LIFE AND LEGACY

Copyright © 2021 by Martha S. Grover

All rights reserved

Published by
Marty Grover Studio
Moultonborough, New Hampshire

ISBN 978-0-578-90578-5

Library of Congress Control Number: 2021916573

All rights reserved. No part of this book may be reproduced or transmitted in any form whatsoever without prior written permission from the Publisher except in the case of brief quotations embodied in critical articles and reviews.

The Memorial program
written by Mary Hadley Case,
a close friend of Tom and Olive Plant
and a member of Bald Peak Colony Club,
seems especially appropriate
to introduce this book.

In Memoriam

Thomas G. Plant

1859 - 1941

I will lift up mine eyes unto the hills, from whence cometh my help. ——Psalms 121:1

Who shall ascend into the hill of the Lord? or who shall stand in his holy place?

He that hath clean hands and a pure heart.
Psalms 24:4-5

A TRIBUTE
TO
A BRAVE HEART

The man for whom this memorial service is held today was known to many of us as the creator of LuckNow and the Bald Peak Country Club. Some of us have memories, reaching back through the years, of a boyish looking man, with white hair, ruddy complexion and blue eyes. A country squire, usually astride a horse. Often he would play a game of golf with us, and we counted our-selves fortunate when he would come into the house with us after the game, and tell us stories of his interesting and varied life.

But not all of us know of the struggle, the courage and daring initiative that brought him from a fourteen-year-old boy who preferred work to school, to the high place as one of the masters of the shoemaking industry.

Concerning his youth, the *Lewiston Journal*, whose editor had known Tom Plant as a boy, had this to say about him:

> "I used to see Tommy Plant play ball.
> He was a catcher — one of the best I
> ever saw. He caught for Fred Reed,
> on the famous old Maumees. He sat
> up behind, or under the bat and picked
> them off bare-handed, without mask
> or shield or mitts or knee guards."

And that is how Thomas Plant went through life; bare-handed, and without mask or shield. He believed that the true test of courage is what a man dares to do *alone*.

His business success is a testimony to this principle. Single-handed he fought and won from a machine monopoly. His victory enabled him to retire from active work and gave him the chance so long waited for, in which to turn to other worthwhile matters.

He had long been a lover of the natural beauty of New Hampshire's mountains, forests and waters.

He was particularly entranced by the magnificent panorama which spreads from the foothills of the Ossipees out over Lake Winnipesaukee to the south. It was here he decided to build his dwelling place and bide his life. With characteristic and dynamic imagination he leveled the top of a mountain and used the rock to construct his house.

At last he had the home of his dreams. He stood on his peak and watched the storms ride by. He saw the glory of the sun's rising and setting and knew that what he had created was good.

After a few years, not content with keeping this beauty spot for himself, he conceived the idea of and built a summer colony on the shore of Lake Winnipesaukee not far from his home. Thus the Bald Peak Country Club came into being, and those of us who were privileged to share this lovely place with him, owe him a debt of gratitude which we can never repay.

He was deeply interested in making life easier to live for his fellow men. He made this interest positive by his gifts to various humanitarian causes. Some of these gifts were known generally to the public, but many of them were known but to few.

He gave to Bath, the place of his birth, an Old Folks Home in memory of his parents; and the inscription (of which he was the author), that was placed upon the wall there, is indicative of his large heartedness toward mankind in general. This inscription reads, "This Home is founded on my sincere belief that those who have lived honest, industrious lives and are without means or friends to care for them, have earned the right to be cared for. Only through the labor and expenditure of others, is it possible for business and professional men to succeed; therefore it is the duty of the strong and successful to care for the deserving aged poor."

During his life at LuckNow he passed the years in doing the things he liked best. He had a love for and knowledge of nature which few of us possess. This brought to him deep pleasure and humble recognition of a divine power which creates and controls all things.

Hunting, fishing, riding over the mountain roads he had built himself, he kept his body exercised and fit, and during the winter evenings, he read history and biography to keep his enquiring mind open and active.

And so he completed his philosophy of life. "Learn to wish things to be exactly as they are." And no adverse blow of fate was able to break the optimism and patience, which together with his courage and originality, were the essence of the man. He believed—

> "All nature is but art, unknown to thee;
> All chance, direction, which thou canst not see;
> All discord, harmony not understood;
> All partial evil, universal good;
> And spite of pride, in erring reason's spite,
> One truth is clear, Whatever is, is right."

Perhaps it is fitting that this brief synopsis of Thomas Plant's life and character should end with his own words:

> "Each day here on my mountain I feel that which nothing else can give me, as I view this beautiful work of nature; and when alone at the top of nature's cathedral, 'my mountain,' surrounded by forests, then I feel through my whole being, the infinite sublime Creator, and the littleness of man."

July twenty-ninth

1941

Written for

my dear friend Olive Plant

in token of

my affection for and my appreciation of

the outstanding qualities

of her beloved husband.

MARY HADLEY CASE

BEGINNINGS IN BATH, MAINE

Thomas Gustave Plant began his life in Bath, Maine on January 5, 1859.[1] By the middle of the 19th century, Bath, situated on the west bank of the Kennebec River, was a flourishing seaport with fortunes being made in the building and sailing of ships of all sizes from yachts to the largest wooden vessels. It became the largest wooden-ship-building city in the world and was surrounded by great forests of oak and spruce to supply the timber for masts and spars.[2] This shipbuilding skill remains as ships continue to be built at Bath Iron Works. Today, the Maine Maritime Academy/Bath Iron Works Apprentice Program in Ship Design and Ship Production is offered only at the Maritime Academy's Bath campus.

It was into this community his parents, Antoine Plante and Sophie Rodrique, who became known as Sophia Roderick and Anton, Antony, Antonio, or Anthony Plant, eventually settled after emigrating from St. Michel, Québec sometime in the 1830's - 1840's. "Antonio" Plant declares in his Federal Naturalization Record (1882) in the state of Maine, he was born "about the middle of February in 1812...at St. Michel, Québec, Canada."[3] It would appear that his French Canadian accent made it very difficult for those recording information in primary resources. For example, Father C. J. O'Callaghan, the pastor of St. Mary's Church in Bath, who baptized both Tom Plant and his younger brother William on February 11, 1863, noted in the church records that Thomas Plant was born in December 1858 the son of Antony Plant and Sophie Ludrique.[4]

Even though Anthony emigrated first to Augusta, Maine in 1834[5], with Sophia following later, he didn't purchase property in Bath until May 24, 1854. In the interim he traveled back and forth to Québec along the Kennebec - Chaudière trail, an ancient path used for centuries by the Indians, French missionaries, famously by Benedict Arnold during the Revolutionary War, and later by immigrants from Québec.

Antoine and Sophie's first child, Joseph L., was born in Québec around 1843. The next two children died in childhood, but the last four lived into adulthood. Frances ("Fannie") was born in Maine in 1857 followed by Tom two years later. William was born four years later in 1863 and the youngest, Agnes, in 1865.

Anthony Plant, described in the land records in 1854 as "laborer," was determined to make Bath his home. He purchased land from John Tucker for $60.00 and built a house in the Tucker Road - Floral Street area commonly called French Hill. However, 1854 was a frightening time in Bath for Québecois and Catholic immigrants. A riotous mob of anti-immigrant, anti-Catholic members of the "Know-Nothing" Native American Party set fire to the Old South Meetinghouse that had been leased to the Roman Catholics in 1847[6]. This secret political party rose to nationwide prominence in the 1850's and elected state and federal officials; nine congressmen, governors, state legislators and thousands of local politicians who shared a fear of immigration.[7]

23 Floral Street, Bath.

The home built by Anthony Plant for his family. Tom Plant was born here in 1859.[8]

Both Anthony and Sophia Plant, who spoke only French when they emigrated to the United States, did learn English, but they were illiterate according to their statements in the Federal Census. Anthony suffered a series of financial reversals requiring him to seek several mortgages in the 1860's and again in the 1880's.[9] In the 1860's he was employed as a fisherman as were a number of his neighbors. However, just a few years later he declared employment as a laborer. Financial salvation arrived with the Civil War. Anthony enlisted in Maine Company F, Seventh Regiment Infantry on January 1, 1862, a month shy of his 54th birthday. This meant a signing bonus and regular pay. His son Joseph Plant enlisted in Bath in June 1863, age 20. He enlisted in Maine Company G, Seventh Regiment after serving in the 12th NH Regiment. His occupation, shoemaker. He, too, would have had a signing bonus and regular pay. His profession was an asset to the military.

The Union soldiers had an advantage over the Confederate soldiers with the availability of shoes and boots. Some think it may have been one of the deciding factors in the outcome of the war.

Sophia and Anthony lived in the Floral Street house until Anthony's death in 1895. In 1896 the house was sold by the heirs of Anthony Plant and the covenant was attested to by Sophia, Joseph L., Thomas G. and Caroline G. Plant, William F. and Margaret V. Plant, Frances D. Kingsbury and Agnes F. and Irvin M. Jordan.[10] Sophia lived the next four years of her life with her daughter, Frances Kingsbury, in Bath. She died on May 5, 1899. The local newspaper reported Tom's repeated trips home to visit his elderly parents. His father was critically ill just before Tom's marriage and died soon after. He was 87 years old.[11]

In 1873, Tom Plant's formal education stopped at the end of the 8th grade when he was fourteen. This was also the year of the Panic of 1873 which triggered the first "Great Depression" both nationally and internationally. This economic downturn lasted for six years. A rush to invest in the railroads across the country led to bond failures and the collapse of banks.[12] Local issuing of railroad bonds in Bath and other infrastructure improvements contributed to Bath's financial debt and enlarged the city's financial obligations at a time when local industry was retrenching. Several other factors contributed to a souring economy in Bath. One was a winter of 12 feet of snow, bringing commerce to a halt.[13] There was a slowdown in the shipyards. Ship construction now was geared toward smaller vessels that were less profitable. And, there were a number of underemployed people in Bath requiring aid. After the Civil War, the national economy remained depressed and morale was too.

Many years later in 1910, The *Bath Independent* newspaper reminisced about the successful hometown boy, Tom Plant, "who was not particularly different from the other boys of that time. Perhaps he had a little more 'ginger' than some and was supplied with a generous quantity of 'grit,' but taken all in all was very much like his playmates." He was athletic - swimming, skating and baseball all appealed to him. "It was always admitted that it made little difference in what game it was, Tom Plant was a hard fellow to beat. He was sandy, determined, perfectly fair and honest, but as one of his old schoolmates expressed it the other day, 'he was an awful digger'! "[14]

Tom Plant Goes To Work

Fourteen years old and sent out to work. It's 1873 and there are a few jobs that require little experience, just grit. Tom Plant tried four of them. His first job was with the shoe manufacturer Cummings & Redman[15] in Bath making $2.50 a week.[16] The next three were associated with Bath's shipping industry — manufacturers of ropes and boilers which also employed some of Tom's neighbors on French Hill.

Cummings & Redman Factory

Rope was a necessary commodity in a ship building community and Bath had several ropewalks for its manufacture. Large sailing ships were rigged with miles of rope, and rigging needed to be replaced regularly. The ropewalk had to be as long as the rope needed for any installation. If the length requirement was longer than the ropewalk, the ropes were fabricated outside. It was heavy work. Natural fibers such as hemp and manila needed to be treated before entering a machine that spun them together to make a cohesive strand. Additional strands twisted together determined the diameter of the rope being made. The twisting process gave rope its strength. The twisted strands alternated from one direction to another for additional size and strength. These ropes were treated with tar for weather protection. Not only was this a dirty job, but there was a very present risk of fire in the ropewalk.

The ice trade provided another source of employment for those willing to work in 30 below temperatures harvesting at least 2 foot thick blocks of ice and storing the blocks in ice houses that lined the river. In its heyday as many as 25,000 men converged on the Kennebec River ice fields.[17] Ice was a luxury commodity and the proximity of the ice to the ships that would carry it made this an efficient product for trade. Ice was shipped south to cities where it was required to cool drinks and keep food cold. Ships returned with coal needed in the north. This seasonal harvest boosted the local economy for many including those families who offered food and lodging to the migrant harvesters.

But, it was his first job that led him to the career he was to follow. Tom's older brother, Joseph, may have introduced him to this career choice. Joseph stated he was a shoemaker when he enlisted in the Union Army in 1863.[18] The William F. Morgan & Co., a shoe manufacturer, had a country shop in nearby Richmond, Maine[19] with a larger presence in Lynn, Massachusetts, a community of shoe manufacturers. Tom worked first in nearby Richmond, lodging with his family before moving to Lynn in 1880 to continue his apprenticeship. In the 1880 Census, Tom and his younger brother William were both living in Lynn, lodging with Mrs. Carol Webster on Friend Street Court, and both identified as shoemakers. Tom was 21 and William, 17.[20] Tom's bench job was as a laster. This had been a completely hand operation but by the 1870's a machine was introduced to draw the shoe upper over the last, center it and hold it by little pincers until the the inner sole could be fastened.[21] A machine could finish the operation in about a minute and a skilled hand laster could only finish 50 shoes in a 10 hour day. Tom was learning the hand method. He moved on to learn the additional skill of edge trimmer to the detriment of his eyesight.

Following a short trip to California to install patent machines, he purchased a covered wagon and sold women's shoes door to door. This was his introduction to market research, and the experience was very valuable. His clients shared their desire for style and smartness as well as durability and economy.[22] This was valuable market information. He was ambitious and determined to start his own business as the owner of a shoe manufacturing company.

Tom Plant was a compact athletic young man, known as one of the best ice skaters around the Bath area.[23] He'd been involved in team sports playing baseball with his Bath friends and gained some personal celebrity as a fearless bare-handed catcher for the famous Old

Maumees[24] and in the 80's, the Bath Blues.[25] By 1875, baseball was firmly rooted in the sporting life of the larger urban communities of the Maritimes and New England. The game was played primarily by adolescents and young men who had only recently entered the work force.[26] Towns and companies fielded teams and the competition was fierce. A little wagering was known to occur. In fact, it was reported that Tom Plant earned the stake he needed to establish his own shoe business by wagering his entire savings on the outcome of a baseball game between the leading Bath team that he captained and a neighboring team. He won![27] But Tom needed more than the stake he had won. He needed experience.

During a strike in 1885, he joined several other shoe workers in organizing a co-operative shoe factory on Eastern Avenue in Lynn, Massachusetts.[28] A few years later Tom Plant withdrew from the co-operative and joined the firm Williams & Clark at 132 Washington Street, Lynn. The firm then became known as Williams, Plant & Co.[29]

Tom and brother William were always very close and both boarded at 6 School Street in Lynn. In 1891, Williams, Plant & Co. moved to 222 Market Street, Lynn. By this time William Plant had married Margaret V. Dobbins.[30] So, for the next several years, Tom lived with William and Margaret at 45 Valley Avenue and later at 73 High Rock Street. During this time all four of William and Margaret's children were born, Amy first, followed by her brothers William, Jr., Thomas, and Everett. Tom maintained a close relationship with his brother's family for the rest of his life.

The Beginnings of a Meteoric Rise

Newspapers around the country found the perfect word to describe Tom Plant's successes. "Meteoric" was how they described his career as shoemaker, businessman and sportsman for the rest of his life.

In 1892, Tom began his own shoe company, located at 463 - 467 Union Street, Lynn.[31] This was a temporary site until he established his business in a larger factory the next year at 685 Washington Street. He remained at this address for the next four years until his final move to Jamaica Plain in 1897. His organization in Lynn was certified June 20, 1893, with a capitalization of $150,000.[32]

Tom Plant was a hard-headed, savvy and determined businessman known for his shrewdness and courage. He was a clear thinker and communicator and others in the industry took notice. He hired men who became management leaders and who remained with the company long after he'd sold his interest and retired. With Tom Plant's leadership, operations went smoothly even as he traveled in England and Europe and across the US to examine newly developed machinery and to search for new markets. The combination of intelligent management with capital and skilled labor was the formula for the company's success.[33] However, there were challenges facing the Company.

A small, one-paragraph article in the *Boston Herald* in February 1892 described a strike in the lasting department of Thomas G. Plant's Lynn Shoe factory. This strike was just the beginning of labor problems that Tom would face in Lynn.

At the end of 1892, Tom joined the committee to prepare for the Lynn Boot and Shoe exhibit for the 1893 Chicago World's Fair. The fair was going to be an important venue for the Thomas G. Plant Company as well as the entire Lynn shoemaking community. It would give Plant a chance to present and promote his Queen Quality lines of shoes and boots throughout the world market.[34] Tom Plant believed that his Queen Quality shoe had superior qualities in its *fitting* and *comfort* and *triumph of quality.*[35] so he needed a symbol that would emphasize those features. He selected Queen Louisa of Prussia.

"Queen Louisa of Prussia, the beautiful and noble woman and queen whose portrait the makers of 'Queen Quality' Shoes have adopted as a symbol of beauty and sterling qualities, has for more than a century held a place in history as a personality rare and perfect."

The World's Fair provided a wonderful platform for Plant, but back at the factory, the labor union demanded higher wages for those employees whose job it was to set edges. This was in late August 1893. By the middle of September all union members were ordered out of the factory. Tom held firm and notified his employees that if the workers wished to be in his employ they would report for work promptly on September 15 or consider themselves discharged. New workmen were hired in all departments and operations gradually resumed.[36] The company announced plans to run a free shop* and secure the help necessary for its business.[37]

---

* A free or open shop is one where union and nonunion workmen are employed without discrimination - union membership is not required for employment.

The World's Fair ended in October and the striking workers in Lynn voted to return to work in December in spite of the opposition of the Knights of Labor leaders. Most were reinstated. They said they'd rather be considered "scabs" than to let their families go without.[38]

Difficulties between management and the unions persisted, but a pleasant diversion for Tom was on the horizon. On June 1, 1895, *The Daily Inter Ocean*, Chicago, published this social event: "Miss Caroline A. Griggs to Wed Mr. Thomas G. Plant of Boston."

Caroline Adams Griggs

"It was while both were abroad that Miss Caroline Griggs became acquainted with Thomas G. Plant, whose career in the shoe manufacturing business had been meteoric. A summer visit of Miss Griggs in Boston later strengthened the friendship begun in Europe."[39]

An elegant marriage ceremony took place at the Lexington Hotel in Chicago on Wednesday, the 26th of June 1895. The Lexington, a residential hotel, had been the home of the Griggs family since they gave up their mansion in Groveland Park. No longer the need for the maid, the cook and the coachman. Samuel Griggs' health had been fragile for some time and life in the hotel was very comfortable.

The decoration of the main parlor with walls lined with palms, doorways and mirrors veiled with asparagus ferns, dotted with LaFrance roses and windows banked with smilax and La France roses describe the grandeur of the venue.

The bride wore cream duchess satin, with a long court train, the waist high and large Bishop sleeves falling to a point over the hand. Her dress and veil were decorated with orange blossoms. We can assume Tom was equally elegant in attire. His best man was Henry F. Colwell, a Boston stockbroker. Caroline was attended by her cousin, Miss Scudder.[40]

Following a wedding breakfast for fifty close friends and family, Tom and Caroline left for New York. They sailed for Europe the following Saturday on the *Campagna* for a honeymoon to last for several months.[41]

Caroline and Tom were in their thirties when they embarked on their marriage. Both were well established in the communities where they lived and Tom's celebrity was world-wide as a result of sharing his name with his very successful shoe company. Caroline or Carrie as she was often called, was wealthy, bright, well-educated, athletic and spoke French fluently. Her parents were from New England, her mother from Rhode Island and her father from Connecticut.

Samuel Chapman Griggs grew up in Hamilton, NY and attended Madison University, now Colgate. He began his career in Hamilton where he started a small country book store. A leading New York publisher, Mark H. Newman, noticed him and offered him a partnership along with financial capital. He proposed a branch in New Orleans, but in those days of slavery, Samuel Griggs, a devout Baptist, couldn't reconcile himself to living in a community based on that social and labor system. He declined the offer. Newman then proposed Chicago for their branch. Samuel Griggs agreed and in 1848 opened a book store as a partner of Mr. Newman in a community that was growing in size and stature to become second only to New York City.

In just a few years, he bought out Newman and became the head of the largest book store in the northwest. Although he'd planned a literary career for himself, his success in building a literary institution in Chicago pleased him. His shop offered many rare and expensive books that were not usually found in a general book store. He traveled to Europe frequently and bought his stock in London, Edinburgh, and Brussels, often the choicest specimens in art and literature alike, the rare and expensive works of older authors and artists, as well as more contemporary works.[42] Unfortunately, he had heavy losses in the great Chicago fire of 1871. His bookstore with its large stock and his home on Michigan Avenue with his valuable library and costly paintings were destroyed.[43] The next year he sold his interest in the book selling business to his partners and began a new and successful career as a publisher.[44]

The Griggses also had a son. Samuel C. Griggs, Jr. was a flashy young man, known in the common parlance of the day as a "dude." Although he invested in several businesses, his interests were in journalism. While working in London on the *Society Times* he contracted pulmonary consumption. A year before his early death at 29, he returned to Chicago and joined his father's publishing company. He had married Mattie Lorimer, the daughter of a prominent Baptist minister, the Rev. Dr. George C. Lorimer, in a quiet wedding in her family home eight years earlier. [45] They had no children.

In 1879, Mattie Lorimer and Caroline Griggs were pursuing their studies at the Lasell Seminary for Young Women, in Auburndale, Massachusetts, a Boston suburb. It was the first junior college for women in the country.[46] After two years at Lasell, Caroline continued her education in New York City. Mrs. Sylvanus Reed's English, French and German Boarding and Day School for young ladies was one of the most prestigious schools for women in New York City, providing the upper crust with a rigorous college-level education not then generally available to women in this country.[47]

Returning to her home in Chicago, Caroline was very active in the social cultural pursuits of Chicago society women. To insure they were as culturally informed and conversationally adept as any New York hostess, the ladies of Chicago began to organize clubs. Caroline belonged to The Cotillion, The Friday Club, The Twentieth Century Club,[48] and, with a group of four friends, began a series of French soirées for the cultivation of French music, literature, and conversation. These soirées were designed for the social and intellectual pleasure that always characterized the French Salon.

In February 1889, the *Chicago Tribune* describes this new offering to society. "A number of ladies of the city who have been so fortunate as to combine refinement with wealth, and who have spent considerable time abroad, especially in Paris, have organized a society, naturally and even necessarily exclusive, for a series of French soirées. An engraved invitation has been sent to the favored few and to only those whose acquirements and standing render them eligible." [49]

With many of her friends, Caroline engaged in a number of philanthropic activities, most of them for the benefit of children. She was a director of a school for young immigrant Italian children and raised funds to support the school by having a number of musical concerts at the Central Music Hall.[50]

A New Focus on Family and Business

Following their honeymoon, Tom returned to his business and a continuation of problems with the unions. A lasters' strike for higher wages began in August while Tom and Caroline were traveling on their honeymoon. The Board of Arbitration of the State of Massachusetts met with both sides and a settlement was reached on Plant's return in October.[51] Through arbitration, he increased the wages of his lasters. This was considered a union victory.[52]

We can only assume Tom and Caroline had a number of conversations about Tom's business concerns and possible solutions to resolve the difficulties with the unions. In the December 31, 1895 issue of the *Boston Journal* there was a small paragraph with a startling bit of news, "Several Shoe Manufacturing Committees in Ohio are bidding for the transfer of the Thomas G. Plant Co's business from Lynn to the West. Mr. Plant has just returned from Cincinnati and expects to move by spring, if thc deal is completed."[53] Was this a shot across the bows of the unions?

Caroline and Tom moved into the Vendome, a residential hotel in Boston's Back Bay. Soon thereafter they moved into The Belvoir, 636 Beacon Street. In setting up housekeeping, they ordered furniture from Herter Brothers. This was a highly regarded company known for fine furniture.[54] The furniture of Herter Brothers represented the pinnacle of American achievement in decorative art and was favored by those with new wealth.[55]

Hotel Vendome. Boston

The Belvoir in 2020

Tom and Caroline spent several weeks at the end of the year visiting her parents at the Lexington Hotel in Chicago. It could be expected that conversations about his business were shared with Samuel and Mary Griggs, also.[56]

By spring, Caroline was planning a diversion. She was an accomplished equestrian and her enthusiasm for the sport was contagious. Tom began his foray into the social realm of the horse show set by acquiring a pair of fine harness horses: Vici and Frenchman and a saddle horse, Brilliant. He exhibited in four classes in the Spring Boston Horse show with success. Tom and Caroline shared a box with the Everett Websters of Lynn during this social event.[57]

In June 1896 a business decision was made. Tom Plant purchased a large tract in Jamaica Plain with a six-story brick factory at the corner of Bickford and Centre Streets.[58]

July found Tom and Caroline enjoying the Oceanside in Gloucester. This may have been the beginning of their summer enjoyment of the North Shore. Perhaps here he found the calm he needed before the storm that arrived after firing the lasters working in the Lynn plant the following month.

The Oceanside and Cottages, Magnolia, Massachusetts

In August he took an unusual step of writing and publishing in the *Boston Daily Advertiser* "The Plant Side" to explain the trouble with the Lasters union at Lynn.

"The Plant Side" as it appeared in the *Boston Daily Advertiser*

"For the past week the newspapers of Lynn and Boston have very harshly criticized the action of the Thomas G. Plant Company for discharging lasters in their employ. An unprejudiced observer could arrive at no other conclusion after reading the papers than that the Thomas G. Plant Company was entirely in the wrong, and very harsh and unfeeling in the treatment of their employees. We feel justified in taking the space to inform the public that we have good and sufficient reason for doing as we have done, We have always employed union lasters.

All the differences that have arisen have been justified by conceding to their demands, which have always been made in the busiest part of our trade. The only exception to the above was one year ago, when their representative demanded a raise of about 15%. The members of the company wished for a few days' time to consider the matter.

About four days later Mr. Carter called again and was notified that during the absence of Mr. Plant, who was in Germany, and who always made and settled all changes in prices, they did not care to assume the responsibility of granting this increase, and requested time to communicate by letter with Mr. Plant, and receive answer by cable.

Mr. Carter absolutely refused to wait the time, and wished them to cable; but, as it would require an expenditure of about $ 300 to cable what was necessary, the firm declined to do so; thereupon Mr. Carter ordered the lasters out on strike, causing us great loss. The strike was prolonged for seven weeks during the busiest part of the season.

Mr. Plant on his return met the full board, but would not attempt settlement with Mr. Carter alone. A compromise was made, and the lasters returned to work. After the meeting Mr. Plant requested Mr. Carter to guarantee that the men would work at the prices fixed upon for the term of one year. This he refused, as he said he could not tell what might arise that would cause dissatisfaction among the lasters. Mr. Plant then claimed unequal liberty, only agreeing that the prices decided upon should continue for one year, provided the work and conditions remained the same.

All agreement that the men or any of them would stay for a year, or that we should employ them for a year, was omitted.

About June 20, we started work at our factory at Ipswich, paying such prices as were paid by manufacturers in the adjoining towns. We soon received numerous calls from the representatives of the Lasters' Union, who wished to force its services upon us in the matter of making prices, and as to whether we should employ union or non-union men.

He was told that the Lasters' Union had no jurisdiction at Ipswich, and that we should act independently of it at the Ipswich factory. Mr. Carter spoke of the dissatisfaction among the hand lasters at our Lynn factory caused by 'their not having work enough, while the machine lasters had all the work they could do.' Mr. Plant advised Mr. Carter to tell the men who were dissatisfied to seek work elsewhere, as it was a matter of choice with them.

Our reasons for keeping the machines busy were that they did the work equal to the hand method, and 10% cheaper, besides enabling the machine lasters to earn more money.

Mr. Carter claimed that it was causing considerable feeling among the men; that something would have to be done to make the distribution of work more equal, whereupon he was again told that those who were dissatisfied should seek work elsewhere, as we were going to put in more lasting machines, and should this season last all work by machine.

He again referred to the Ipswich matter, and demanded a more satisfactory answer as to our intentions in dealing with the Lynn Lasters' Union at Ipswich, to which we replied as before, stating that Ipswich was not in Lynn, therefore, we would not be dictated to by the Lynn Lasters' Union as to our methods of doing business at Ipswich 'Then you defy us' was the reply; to which question he was answered that he could understand it as he pleased.

They immediately petitioned the General Board of the Boot and Shoe Workers' Union not to grant a charter to Ipswich, but to give them jurisdiction over the factory at Ipswich. At their next meeting, they received a communication from the General Board of the Boot and Shoe Workers' Union granting their request, and giving them jurisdiction over Ipswich.

At this time we were lasting shoes at Ipswich by the method of team work, of four men and a machine operator dividing the work into parts which has heretofore been done by one man, enabling the men to turn out more work, and reducing the cost of producing the shoe, while at the same time enabling them to earn as much money as by the old method.

These men were paid from $13 to $18 per week, according to ability, which is all that the same men could earn were they working by the piece in other factories at the old method.

Having decided to introduce the Ipswich system in the Lynn factory, we were aware that the Lasters' Union would not recognize this method of doing work, and knew that as soon as they could get a hold in our Ipswich factory they would cause a strike, or could they not gain a hold they would order out the Lynn lasters to force us to their terms, and we as well as the Lasters' Union were prepared for the trouble, it being simply a question who would first openly take the aggressive, and as soon as we ascertained that they had gained Ipswich under the Lynn jurisdiction, and that one of the prominent officers of the Boot and Shoe Workers' Union had been detailed to go to Ipswich to organize, we decided to seek lasters that would last our shoes in Lynn by the same method that we were using in Ipswich, as we knew it was only a matter of a few days when the Lynn lasters would be called out; hence the necessity of protecting ourselves by discharging our lasters, as the conditions made it impracticable for us longer to deal with the Lasters' Union.

Under the agreement our men were at perfect liberty to leave our employment if they desired, and we were equally at liberty to discharge them if we chose.

We have not violated any agreement made with the Lasters' Union, yet they have persistently stated that we have. Had the Lasters' Union avoided interfering with our Ipswich work, however, this trouble would never have arisen.

Mr. Carter called on us and was told by Mr. Plant that when the lasters were discharged all connection between the Thomas G. Plant Company and the Lynn Lasters' Union ceased, and that in the future they would not recognize the Lasters' Union and would only deal with the men they employed.

We are willing to employ the same lasters to work the new method adopted, paying them by the week as much as they have averaged during the past season.

We have paid out in Lynn the past spring season nearly $ 250,000 for labor, which certainly shows that our employees are not ground down by a despot. The fact that the larger part of the employees of the Thomas G. Plant Co. have been with us year after year proves that they are fairly dealt with, both as to prices and treatment, a record not at all compatible with the charge laid at our door during the present trouble.

Employment has always been and always will be open, when we have work to offer, to all good workmen irrespective of their being union or non-union, but we do not concede that organized labor has a mortgage on all the positions in our factory, or any right to dictate to us whether we shall employ union or non-union men. Should they ever gain any such right or authority, then the Thomas G. Plant Co. will retire from business."

Thomas G. Plant Co. [59]

If he'd been hoping to quell opposition to the firing of the lasters, he'd missed the mark. In August most of his employees walked out in sympathy with the lasters. Non-union lasters were brought in from Maine and New York and fed and housed in the factory. Preparations were made to move the cutting and stitching departments to a newly leased Ipswich factory to ease the antagonism of the labor union men in Lynn.

Finally, Tom Plant petitioned the Superior Court and an injunction was granted to prevent the intimidation of those who desired to work in the factory.[60] The result of this action by the Thomas G. Plant Shoe Company was one of the largest labor demonstrations ever held in Lynn. A parade was formed of representatives of almost all the prominent labor organizations in the city and included five bands and 2,500 union members marching with banners streaming. The crowd was estimated at 20,000. There was a heavy police presence. The main holdout union was the Knights of Labor who represented the cutters. James J. Dolan, an official of the Knights of Labor wrote a public letter condemning the Boot and Shoe Workers' Union for bringing about the strike and driving the shoe business from Lynn.[61] The Boot and Shoe Workers' Union was very bitter at their lack of support of the strike.[62]

The Company successfully added enough workers to run full-time and by November the strikers declared they'd had enough and petitioned the company to see if they would be taken back. The Boot and Shoe Workers' Union was bitterly opposed to acknowledging defeat.[63] In December, workers in all departments were sought for the new plant in Jamaica Plain, a Boston suburb. Operations began and the Lynn plant was leased. The ads for shoe workers were a daily feature in the newspapers: tip stitchers on zigzag machines, McKay stitchers, foxing stitchers, sidestep stitchers, vampers, edge trimmers, lining makers, closers on Wilcox & Gibbs eyeletters; lasters, both hand and on Boston tacker, sole layers and first-class skivers, "none other need apply." In fact many of these ads began, "First-class"...wanted and ended, "none other need apply."

December 31, 1896, the Board of the Thomas G. Plant Shoe Company formally signed an Indenture to lease the shoe plant from Tom Plant for $14,000. a year over a ten year period.[64] This allowed Tom to pay off the mortgage that he'd acquired from the Lynn Safe Deposit and Trust Company by the middle of January 1897.[65]

The Thomas G. Plant Shoe Company announced in the January 4, 1897 issue of the *Boot and Shoe Recorder* that the business has been "entirely removed from Lynn to Boston. Therefore the trade is requested to take particular note of the fact that all correspondence, packages, express or freight matter should be sent to the Thos. G. Plant Co., corner of Centre and Bickford streets, Station T, Boston, Mass."

By the September 22 issue, the *Boot and Shoe Recorder* provides its readers with their view of the Plant Company -

"Why The Thomas G. Plant Company

> does such an enormous business is not at all strange to those acquainted with the company's methods. They are of the most up-to-date description, and involve the making of goods which women of today are calling for, and which they are enabled to buy. 'Popular-priced, stylish, natty goods,' represents briefly, the Thomas G. Plant Co. lines in McKays and welts, and their popularity is well attested by the fact that the great Boston factory is now turning out close to five thousand pairs daily. No factory in the country turns out so many $2 and $2.25 boots for women's wear as the Plant Company. And the company has the best equipped shoe factory today in America."

The Original Thomas G. Plant Shoe Company in Jamaica Plain

"Chicago, April 6 [1897] - Samuel C. Griggs, one of the pioneer book publishers of the West, died last night. For many years he has been prominent in the book business and leaves a large fortune."[66] The *Chicago Tribune* posted a lengthy obituary and history of this pioneer of Chicago. Griggs had been frail for some time and a year before his death had suffered a stroke and paralysis. With her father's death, Caroline rushed to Chicago to be with her mother.

In July, Mrs. Griggs joined Caroline and Tom for the "pure air and water" of Lake Massapoag in Sharon, Massachusetts, a spring fed 350 acre lake twenty miles southwest of Boston. The Lake Massapoag Hotel offered 100 rooms with modern conveniences as well as livery stables, tennis courts, croquet, billiards, pool, boating, hunting and fishing. In addition, there were lectures, programs, and even a hotel orchestra. It became their summer residence.[67] The following July they all returned to Lake Massapoag and Mrs. Griggs stayed on for part of the fall at the Vendome in Boston, where Caroline and Tom had their apartment.

Tom's mother, Sophia Plant, died in May. She had been living with her daughter, Mrs. Joseph Kingsbury in Bath since the death of her husband in 1895. This native of Montreal had been in poor health for several years. Her funeral service was attended by all five of her surviving children and their spouses and a large group of friends.[68] She was buried next to her husband in the Maple Grove Cemetery in Bath.

Social Notes

That summer Tom and Caroline and Caroline's mother left the lake for the sea. They were guests at the Masconomo for the season in Manchester-by-the Sea.[69]

Tom and Caroline expanded their sporting endeavors and traveled to the Rangeley Lake House in Rangeley, Maine in June 1900 where they rented a cottage for the fishing.[70] The society pages of the *Boston Herald* include them in the coverage of the Boston Horse Show in April 1901 and in June with fellow anglers at The Birches in Maine. By July, they and Mrs. Griggs were back at the Masconomo, one of the Gilded Age's most famous summer resort hotels.[71] [72]

Even with the demands of a growing business and the threat of lawsuits, the Plants maintained an active social life. In January 1902,

Caroline participated in the first of a series of afternoon concerts given by the Symphony Orchestra at the Tuileries for the benefit of the Tyler Street Day Nursery.[73] She continued to sponsor the same type of fund-raising programs to benefit the needs of children that had interested her in Chicago.

April of 1902 found Tom and Caroline making a pleasure tour of the West Coast and staying in an apartment at the Palace in San Francisco while they toured. [74]

Then on June 24, they sailed from Boston to Liverpool, England aboard the Cunard steamer Ivernia ensconced in one of its first class saloons.[75]

S.S. IVERNIA, 1900 Cunard Line
Courtesy The Peabody Museum of Salem

Close to the end of August, the Masconomo announces that "Mr. Thomas G. Plant of Boston, the well known shoe manufacturer, and family are at the Masconomo House."[76]

According to the column "Table Gossip" in the November 1, 1903 *Boston Globe*, "Mr. and Mrs. Thomas G. Plant have given up their Beacon Street apartment and will be at the Somerset for the winter."

Hotel Somerset, Boston

"Social Notes" in the April 10 *Sunday Boston Herald* mentions "Mrs. Thomas G. Plant, an all-round horsewoman, has been doing much riding and driving this winter. Mrs. Plant, who with her husband is at present in the South, will be one of the most regular attendants at the horse show, where Mr. Plant is numbered among the exhibitors. They are returning to Boston this week in order to be here at the opening of the show."[77]

In the April 1903 Boston Horse Show at the Mechanics' Building, Tom Plant exhibited his favorite saddle horse Sunshine and his trotter Alice Carr and roadsters Brilliant and Ebony Boy. That year, Reginald Vanderbilt brought a large string of horses up from New York and left the Boston show with a basket full of blue ribbons. At the end of September, the Annual Breeders' Meeting and Horse Show brought much more satisfaction for Tom. Ebony Boy won the blue in the Roadster class, and Animation and Sunshine brought home the first and second prize in the Saddle class.

"Social Notes" again brings us up to date with the Plants' equestrian activities as it has been reported that Mr. and Mrs. Thomas G. Plant are sailing for Europe on the Saxonia. They planned to be absent a few months while coaching with friends in England.[78]

In 1904, Mrs. Griggs left her home in the Hotel Lexington in Chicago and moved into an apartment in the Hotel Somerset, Boston where her daughter and son-in-law also have an apartment. She was 82 years old.

RMS *Saxonia*

An Enlightened Industrialist

Because of the difficulties with the unions, Tom Plant believed that his new factory would run more smoothly and more effectively if he provided a better working environment. He believed that it was good business policy to improve the health and well-being of the workers. "A workman who knows when he is well off, prefers not to strike; an employer who is making money, prefers to keep things going smoothly."[79]

"That belief led to the completion in 1903 of a company program to improve the health, security, and relationships with the company's employees. Profit sharing was introduced, sick and death benefits and a savings fund department was instituted to encourage frugal and industrious behavior on the part of the employees.

"A new six-story addition was built adjoining the current factory on Centre Street and opened the first week in January. Its purpose was to give the employees a place to improve their minds and bodies. A gymnasium was on the 25,000 square foot first floor. Equipment included specially built apparatus that could be moved away to give floor space for class work. Each session accommodated 60 with 60 separate showers and dressing rooms. Gym work was the charge of one of the best professional instructors in the country. A woman instructor from the Boston Normal School of Gymnastics drilled the participants in her classes. The gym is the same size as the Y.M.C.A. on Boylston Street and is provided with a running track of equal size.

"On the second floor there is a billiard and game room for the special use of the foremen, and a general billiard and game room and bowling alleys for the other employees. There is the library and reading room, open at all times and attended by a librarian. The library is a branch of the public library of Boston with a large circulation of books and magazines. There's a lunch room which supplies clean healthful food at the actual cost of preparation. There is also a private room, decorated with carpeting and pictures that gives the women who do piece work a place to rest away from their work stations. A large recreation room with a player piano gives a space for meetings, lectures and dances.

"There is also a room where medical assistance can be found should a worker become ill or injured in the factory. The company also provides two free beds at the Emergency Hospital and all cases requiring surgical attention are taken there at no charge to the patient."[80]

In April 1904, the *Boston Herald* reported on a Company-sponsored employee dance evening. "If an employee of a shoe factory had been brought to an entertainment such as that given last night by the Thomas G. Plant Company at their factory, Centre and Bickford streets, Roxbury, he would scarcely have believed his eyes. Most employees in a shoe factory are glad enough to leave as soon as the whistle blows at night and not return again until called back to the machines in the morning, but here, at 9 PM there were nearly 1,500 employees. The click of the machines, however, had given place to the strains of the Queen Quality band, and work-a-day clothes had been changed for Sunday best. Downstairs the bowling alleys and pool tables were busy, in other rooms the older people were enjoying whist, and up on the top floor the shoe cases had been cleared away and a ballroom extemporized. Flags had been hung along all sides of the walls, suspended in clusters from the ceiling, palms had been brought in. The concert lasted until 10, and then Mr. Ernest Hermann took charge of the floor and directed the dancers. Fully 100 couples participated and there were nearly 300 more looking on. During the intermission in the dancing, a short program consisting of readings, magic and music was rendered and the dancing was resumed until 12. Among the members of the firm present were Vice-President, W. F. Plant, Treasurer William L. Ratcliffe, Supt. W. J. McGaffee, Directors W. A. Mitchell and J. H. Brock."[81]

This view of Tom's business acumen appeared in an article in the September 21, 1901 *Boston Herald* which described the business decisions of the shoe company.

The Boston Herald

"The Thomas G. Plant Company, manufacturers of the famous 'Queen Quality' shoes, has reduced the working day of their 2,000 employees to eight hours.

"Two years ago the Plant company with a pay pool of $1,000,000 per annum decided to adopt the nine-hour system. They believed that, under proper conditions, their factory could produce as many shoes with the nine-hour system as with the usual 10-hour shoe factory day. By adopting special methods in keeping the help employed, requiring promptness in attendance, the new departure was made a success in results, and recently it was decided to still further reduce the hours to eight instead of nine.

"This is the outcome of a perfect system in supervising every detail of an immense business. Today the Thomas G. Plant Company enjoys the unique distinction of having voluntarily put into effect an eight-hour system without any change at all being made in the wages of their week hands, which is one-fifth of their total force employed, and further, the company claims that under conditions now enforced the piece work help can earn as much in the eight-hour day as they formerly earned in the 10-hour day.

"The equipment of the factory is well-nigh perfection. There are separate entrances for male and female employees, with three elevators to carry the latter to their respective floors. Hat and coat lockers are provided for all. Water boys are constantly in attendance to supply fresh drinking water to those who want it. Within the factory sanitary arrangements are of the very best. The system of ventilation is perfect. During the months when the windows are necessarily kept closed, there are 24 large ventilating fans kept running to exhaust the impure air, which is replaced by pure air from an immense blower. Under such conditions it is not surprising to find efficiency, harmony and earnings per capita averaging higher than other and less advantageously planned and conducted establishments.

"It is the company's belief that when a dispute is verging on a strike the principals involved are not competent to decide fairly which side is right. It is only the impartial third party who can do so. To carry this belief into effect, the Plant company has bound itself by a signed agreement with each employee, whereby any grievance not satisfactorily adjusted between the employees and the firm shall be submitted to the Board of Arbitration and Conciliation of the Commonwealth of Massachusetts, whose decision shall be final and binding on both."

Tom's philanthropy did not go unnoticed in Bath. The *Bath Daily Times,* his hometown newspaper delighted in reporting what the "Two Bath Boys" were doing to benefit their fellow man: Tom was building a new six-story brick building adjoining the present immense factory to provide the space for recreational and instructive programs for his workers. His chief thought was for the improvement of mind and body of his employees. His plan was to keep this building open until 10 o'clock each night and it was certainly going to be a boon for all the workers who lived in single rooms in local boarding houses. The employees were very excited at the prospect of this novel idea. This was only the beginning of his construction plans at the factory site. The company had just purchased an adjoining tract of land for a new building devoted exclusively for the manufacture of shoes which will increase the manufacturing space to double his output and increase the number of employees to 5,000.[82]

Tom Plant, as the chief executive of the company, retained complete supervision, giving his personal attention to all important matters of policy. All those holding responsible positions, having been identified with the Thomas G. Plant Co. since its beginning had become experts in their several departments, which they manage in such a way that the entire establishment moves as a unit; a very vital item and one that any business man would appreciate.[83] This structure provided Tom with the freedom to pursue all his many interests.

It is clear that his employees were important to Tom. He and his private secretary, Alfred Handley, opened the "Noonday Rest Park" May 27, 1910 with a band concert and promenade. The park was planted on a former factory dumping site of about 160,000 square feet. Tom and Alfred Handley conceived the idea the preceding winter and with the direction of the Olmsted Brothers[84] firm made an attractive park for the employees. It contained three ovals, two for relaxation and one for athletic pursuits. It was enthusiastically embraced by the employees. One hundred and twenty-five large shade trees and 9,000 shrubs of all varieties were imported and placed along the walks. At the rear of the park a 100x40 foot greenhouse grew fresh flowers and plants and fresh flowers were regularly delivered to the female employees. In the park, benches were installed to provide seating for 1,200 and the park was enclosed by an iron fence supported by stone posts.[85]

The Noonday Rest Park was very popular during the lunch hour. For those who wished an extended view of the area, there was a roof promenade, protected with heavy iron railings around the coping, covering two thirds of the roof. From this vantage point, views of Boston and the blue hills of Milton could be enjoyed.

" Noonday Rest Park"

The Bath Independent

On June 4, 1910 Bath, Maine's hometown newspaper, *The Bath Independent* lauded Tom with the following headline —

"World's Greatest Shoe Manufacturer. Thomas G. Plant, a Bath Born Man, Heads the Largest And Finest Establishment on Earth - Description of The Model Factory Which Employs Thousands of Busy Workers."

The details of the efficient design of the factory most likely came from Tom in an interview with his hometown newspaper.[86]

"The factory is built in form of a hollow square, with rear and side wings on both Centre and Bickford streets, and a side overlooking the private park owned by the company. The building is of brick throughout built in accordance with the most approved methods of factory construction and really comprises ten buildings under one roof.

"The building is six stories in height, with basement. The uniform width is 52 feet and the total length, if each room were placed end to end would be one and seven-eights miles, with a total floor space of 13 acres.

"In addition to being the largest shoe making establishment in the world it is the most perfectly equipped, both from a manufacturing and sociological standpoint. The building is thoroughly equipped with automatic sprinklers and well protected by water supplies, such as reservoirs, overhead tanks, three separate water mains and large fire pumps.

"The boiler house, which is detached from the main building, contains five 350 horse-power boilers, equipped with fuel stokers; it has a radial brick chimney, 150 feet high and consumes annually 9,000 tons of coal; there are nine engines and five generators.

"The roof is of sawtooth skylight construction, with northern exposure, to ensure a soft, clear light, so necessary for the cutting and upper fitting departments, which occupy the upper floors.

"The system of supplying fresh air for all departments is as nearly perfect as human ingenuity can devise or desire - 53 large fans and blowers are employed, requiring 350 horse-power to operate. The building is heated and ventilated by direct air circulation system ensuring a constant supply of fresh air.

"To ensure an equalized temperature throughout the big building during the cold season, upwards of 70 thermometers and numerous hygrometers are located throughout the factory, and also used to regulate the humidity of the air." The proper humidity was extremely important for the storage of leather used in production. The quantity of hides consumed to make 17,000 pairs of shoes daily were the hides and skins of 9,350 kids and goats, 500 horses and colts, 1,600 calves and 975 steers.

"The sanitary equipment is as good as the best hotels. All lavatories are fitted with sanitary plumbing of the most approved type, with floors of vitrified ceramic tiles and are scrupulously clean. No unnecessary dust is created during working hours: all sweeping and cleaning is done at night, when the building receives a thorough and systematic cleaning by an efficient corps of janitors. Tobacco chewing is prohibited."[87] There was more, much more about the efficiency of the plant and the concern for the smooth operation of a business employing 5,500 workers. There was a central telephone system connecting every department with eight trunk lines and 55 individual telephones. Included were a Western Union and Cable office. Packages as large as 10" x 20" were delivered to the end of each floor by way of a Lamson lift. Two messengers per floor delivered packages on roller skates to speed delivery.

"Recognizing that if operators are to earn the maximum wages they must be required to leave their work as little as possible, the cutting room is provided with endless carriers for transporting the patterns, thereby greatly reducing the unproductive time. The upper fitting departments are arranged in a novel manner, making it easy to supply work and care for the 1,500 operatives there. Electric push buttons connecting with annunciators enable the operatives to call for and be supplied with work or the services of a machinist or boy to attend to their wants. The upper stitching work is carried from one department to another by a system of carrier belts. Lasts withdrawn from the shoes upon different floors in remote parts of the factory are automatically returned to the starting point for re-use."[88]

There was a pneumatic tube pick-up and delivery system throughout the plant used to deliver small items, primarily paychecks.

The plant provided locked boxes for personal tools and lockers for changes of clothes and a cloak room for outside clothing and umbrellas. The personal care of each employee extended not only to the skilled physician on staff but also to an "oculist" to inspect eyesight and provide corrective glasses if needed. His fee was free and the glasses were provided at cost.

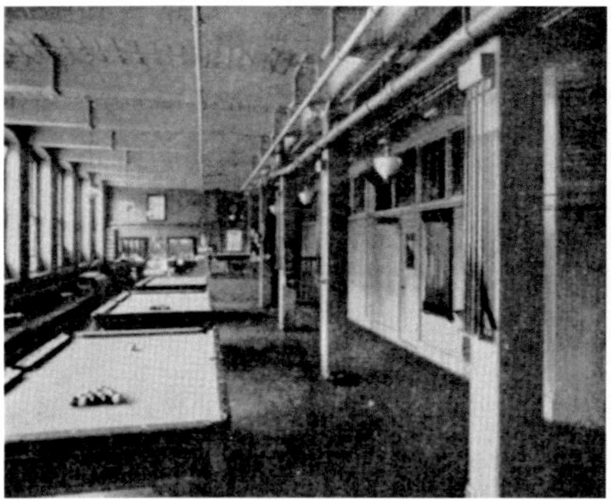
The Billiard Hall

The Dance Hall

Cutting room with new incandescent lamps with Halophane glass and steel reflectors

The Changing World of Shoe Manufacture

The world of shoe manufacturing was undergoing such significant change that the entire industry would be impacted. On February 10, 1899 a corporation was organized in New Jersey with a capital of $25,000,000 that would change shoe machinery leases for most shoe manufacturing businesses. This corporation, United Shoe Machinery Company, consisted of all the shoe machinery businesses of any magnitude.[89]

In July 1899 there was a push-back by a number of shoe manufacturers who formed their own combination of shoe machinery companies into the Standard Shoe Machinery Company with a capital stock of $5,000,000 whose purpose was to offer less expensive leases. Tom Plant was vice president of the Standard.[90]

Shoe manufacturers met in Philadelphia in August, 1899 to form the National Shoe Manufacturers' Association. Increased costs were the concern. Leasing costs and material costs, particularly leather prices, were going up and manufacturers wanted to be able to guarantee prices for the coming season.[91] Tom Plant was named First Vice President of the newly elected board of directors adding to the complexities of his very busy life.

An announcement in the business news in July 1901; The Thomas G. Plant Company, makers of boots and shoes, has been incorporated in New Jersey with a capital of $2,500,000.[92]

In the summer of 1901, The Standard Shoe Machinery Company reorganized into The American Consolidated Shoe Machinery Company because one of the original participating companies, Bay State, wished to withdraw and was now owned by United Shoe Machinery Company. This was just another skirmish in the shoe machinery business world.[93]

Some years later, in 1922, Frederick J. Allen explained the growth of the shoe industry, in his book *The Shoe Industry*, stating that the standardization of machinery and service from the leasing companies leveled the playing field between large and small manufacturers. There could be as many as 174 machine operations using 154 different machines involved in the manufacturer of high quality women's shoes. The ability to lease these machines from a company that would also maintain them enabled newcomers to compete.

An important piece of news was noted during the Pan-American Exposition that was held in Buffalo, New York between May and November 1901. That news was the award of the Gold Medal for the "Queen Quality Shoe" produced by the Thomas G. Plant Shoe Company. The award noted a superior shoe that combined all the essentials of the finest footwear and could be produced at a cost that would permit its being retailed at $3.00 a pair.[94] (President William McKinley was fatally shot at the Exposition on September 6th. He was succeeded by the Vice President, Theodore Roosevelt.)

As United Shoe Machinery patents on individual machines began to expire, shoe manufacturers, including Tom Plant, began to improve the equipment with their own modifications. Tom had a quick and inventive mind and as he improved machinery, he took out patents. While this method of improving the shoe machinery had been an accepted method of operating in the past, the United Shoe Machinery Company decided to fight what they considered to be patent infringement.[95] Consequently, patent infringement cases against the Thomas G. Plant Shoe Company by the United Shoe Machinery Company began to come to the courts. More about this important battle between the well established United Shoe Machinery Company and the rising challenger will be presented in subsequent chapters.

Wanting to build his business at Jamaica Plain, Plant initiated one of the most interesting advertising campaigns in 1902. It was the introduction of the Dorothy Dodd brand, a shoe manufactured by the "Dorothy Dodd Shoe Company of Boston." Interestingly, there was no mention of the Thomas G. Plant Shoe Company associated with this new brand. A very clever introduction was made in several magazines. The advertisement displayed in *Munsey's Magazine* is shown on the following pages.

The True Story of Dorothy Dodd.

DOROTHY DODD was clever and original — a girl of ideas, with a good head for business, yet withal charmingly feminine. She had a pretty, stylish figure and was *always* dressed in such faultless taste that her friends thought whatever Dorothy wore must be right.

Not only were her hats and gowns *always* perfection, but she showed the characteristics of a true Parisienne in her fastidiousness about her gloves and shoes, the latter always being the most up-to-date.

Dorothy possessed too strong an individuality, too positive a character to continue to be satisfied with the purposeless existence of the average girl in her sphere.

For some time she had been trying to decide what work she would most enjoy doing, and how she could best gratify her great desire to do something which would benefit her own sex. The result of her deliberation was the conclusion that she would like to be a business woman.

Now Dorothy for a long time had designed her own shoes and had had them made for her by a prominent shoe manufacturer, because it had been her experience in purchasing them that whenever she had a pair that satisfied her in appearance, they invariably wrinkled or pinched somewhere. These frequent misfits finally resulted in the ultra-fastidiousness Miss Dorothy being obliged to admit the possession of a corn. To insure comfort and at the same time please her critical eye and exquisite taste, she had become the designer of her own shoes in every detail.

Thinking over her wonderful success in designing her shoes, she felt she could do much for other women by giving them the benefit of her ideas. So in choosing a business this fact decided her and she enthusiastically exclaimed "It shall be shoes: shoes better than all other shoes; shoes that are stylish and beautiful; shoes that shall not pinch; in short, shoes like no other shoes in the world," and shoes it was.

When Dorothy had come to a decision, people who knew her knew that something was sure to come of it.

In this particular instance she lost no time in seeking her father's assistance in carrying her ideas into effect and at her request he sought the shoe manufacturer who made her shoes and who had one of the best equipped factories in America. This manufacturer had been greatly impressed with Dorothy's ability in designing her own shoes and had often secretly wished that her original ideas about shoes could be used in his business, so when Dorothy's father told him of his daughter's desires, he quickly saw the advantage of utilizing her unusual ability, and after some thought, concluded to form a company under her name, in which she was to be a most important factor, and this is how it came about that the Dorothy Dodd Shoe Company was formed.

The most expert makers of patterns and lasts were called into service, the most skilled workmen were employed, and when these helpers had applied themselves enthusiastically to carry out Miss Dorothy's original ideas, the result was the "faultless fitting" Dorothy Dodd Shoe.

In the next issue of this publication, Dorothy Dodd will tell of her experience in shoe designing and what is meant by "a faultless fitting shoe." Although Dorothy is a reality, this is not her real name, but her name has in it all the letters which form "Dorothy Dodd." Very truly yours.

Dorothy Dodd Shoe Company,

Manufacturers, BOSTON, MASS.

Lest anyone forget Queen Quality shoes, the Company offered $5,000 in prize money to 100 women for the best reasons why the "Queen Quality" shoe is superior to all other shoes. The first prize was $1,000. The contestants numbered in the thousands and represented all parts of the country. Dealers selling Queen Quality shoes supplied the forms for the contest. The contest was open from October 1 to December 25, 1902.[96] Soon, a similar contest was offered by the Dorothy Dodd Shoe Company for a total prize money of $4,000.

The Sporting Life

Sunshine, Tom's favorite saddle horse began a successful 1903 season in April's Boston Horse Show. By May, Tom's interest moved to the development of the Charles River Speedway and to racing at the Readville Trotting Park. In August his trotter Brilliant was having great success. Also in August, Tom bought Richard Healey's great driving horse, Comet for $2,500, an offer so great that Healey found he couldn't refuse it.[97] Tom's horses; His Highness, Dee Jay, Crowshade and Comet were also being campaigned at the Park.[98] October found his trotters; Alice Carr, His Highness and Comet winning races at the Trotting Park.[99]

Readville Trotting Park

At the Annual meeting of the Algonquin Club in November, Tom was voted onto the executive committee.[100] He and his racing friends, many of whom belonged to the Algonquin, were planning a club house for the Boston Gentlemen's Driving Club.

Now that racing was forbidden in Brookline, many drivers who had enjoyed racing on the Beacon Street road were visiting the Charles River Speedway for the first time at the end of December. They were pleasantly surprised by the conditions of the racing road that was provided and maintained by the state along the banks of the Charles River in North Brighton. The construction of the club house for the Speedway was almost complete. W. W. Dinsmoor was the architect and

Tom Plant and some of the other members were involved in the funding of the construction.

The club house and stable were built in just four weeks and cost $15,000. The stable provided accommodations for over 50 horses and also made a very comfortable home for the club members during the winter months.[101]

Architect's sketch for the Gentlemen's Driving Club House

(Photo by Post Photographer.)
THOMAS G. PLANT BEHIND HIS HANDSOME MARE, ALICE CARR, WHO HAS CAPTURED THREE BLUE RIBBONS IN THE BOSTON DRIVING CLUB CHAMPIONSHIP SNOW SPEEDING CLASS THIS SEASON, AND IS KNOWN AS THE QUEEN OF THE SPEEDWAY.

An interesting article appeared in the *Boston Post* on January 19, 1904, "Mr. and Mrs. Thomas G. Plant figured in an exciting runaway on the Brighton speedway yesterday afternoon.

"Incidentally, the spectators witnessed one of the grittiest and cleverest pieces of horsemanship seen on the speedway this season.

"Mr. Plant, the well-known shoe manufacturer, was driving his pair of geldings, Ebony Boy and His Highness. Beside him sat Mrs. Plant, enveloped in furs.

"As Mr. Plant was sending them down the track at a lively gait yesterday the horses became unmanageable, and broke into a wild run that made the onlookers shudder.

"Try as he might, Mr. Plant could do nothing to stop the speed of the spirited animals. His hands were fast losing their grip, and a smashup with serious consequences seemed to be certain, when Mrs. Plant, who is an expert horsewoman, instead of swooning with fright, came to the rescue.

"Throwing her fur cape from her shoulders in a business-like way, she stood up in the sleigh, and, grasped the reins firmly with both hands.

"Then she pulled evenly and steadily until she had taken up enough slack in the reins to permit her to regain her seat.

"Mrs. Plant was showered with congratulations by friends and strangers alike." [102]

The *Boston Journal* reported on April 17, 1904 that Caroline Plant was in the south and was expected to return to her apartment in the Somerset after a visit to Atlantic City where she'd spent some time. She would return before the Boston Horse Show later in the month.

Horse shows and racing occupied Tom again this year and a particularly interesting event was the first Speedway parade in June. Alice Carr won the half-mile record and Tom's black pair, Ebony and Brilliant, were an attractive team that gained notice out of over 300 teams which took part in the parade. The participants comprised the most prominent gentlemen drivers of Boston who were admired for their horses and appointments.

Notice of a totally different form of locomotion was made in the July 7, 1904 *Boston Herald* with the headline "**Boston Auto's Good Run**." The article, dated July 6, 1904, Bethlehem, NH "Thomas G. Plant and R. R. Ross of Boston left on Monday at 8 AM for the White Mountains by way of Concord, North Woodstock and Franconia Notch in a 22-horse power touring car. At the Weirs they were joined by Miss Plant (niece Amy) and took on 250 pounds of baggage. They reached the Sinclair, Bethlehem at 8 o'clock, the time being 12 hours, including stops for meals. Less than 12 gallons of gasoline were consumed on the trip, which was made without accident. They are making some runs over the mountain roads and return to Boston Thursday by way of Crawford Notch, Ossipee and Rochester."

1904 22 hp Packard Touring Car.

Note: R. R. Ross was the agent in Boston for Packard and Cadillac cars.

A member of the American Motor League observed, "Motoring is a disease for which there is no panacea except more motoring."

Although Tom was busy with his horses throughout the season, which ended in December with racing at the Speedway, the company was growing and the factory expanding. A photo of a new addition, built in only 46 days in 1904 was shown in *The Shoe Retailer*, Vol. 52, dated January 11, 1905.

Addition to Thomas G. Plant Shoe Factory, Boston

March and April 1905 found Tom and Caroline again in the south for the Annual Horse Show. They stayed at the Kenilworth Inn in Asheville, NC.[103] Lady Pearson of England and Mrs. George W. Vanderbilt awarded the prizes. Many prominent society people from New York and Philadelphia including Mrs. Beekman Lorillard and Frederick W. W. Graham of Philadelphia, President of the Horse Show Association participated in the show. "Four prizes, including the two Vanderbilt cups, were won by Thomas G. Plant of Boston."[104] One could imagine the Vanderbilts planned some social events at their nearby 250 room French Renaissance chateau, Biltmore, during the show. This wonderful "summer home" was completed in 1895 after 7 years of construction. It had the distinction of being the largest private residence in the country at the height of the Gilded Age.

In May, Caroline Plant introduced her own horses at the Brookline Country Club Horse Show. In the saddle class (side saddle for ladies) she won with her champion mare, Sunlight. She also won the ladies amateur event for runabouts with her handsome coal black gelding, Firefly, and in another event paired him with her black mare, Flashlight. In the Lady's phaeton horse event she received high commendation with her mare Irene. Later in a novice harness class, she paired Irene with Iris. In still another class for pair horses she won the blue ribbon with Brilliant and Ebony Boy. Her costume for the closing of the show was described as white, with a white turban, blue plumes.[105]

Mrs. Plant's Blue Ribbon Winner, Firefly

Tom had a great interest in both horses in harness and, following his trip with his niece and R.R. Ross, in travel by automobile.

In October 1905 he, Caroline, and Mrs. Griggs made a motoring trip through part of Canada.[106] His automobile was most likely a new Packard, a car with a wonderful reputation for style and comfort.

Packards 1905 Model N was a very up to date automobile by a company that at this point in time was quite progressive and building very high quality cars. In 1904 they establish-ed the distinctive Packard radiator shape, that would be their trademark until the end in the fifties.

In support of his equestrian pursuits, he purchased Dr. Reid for $1,450 at Fasig-Tipton sale at Madison Square Garden in November, 1906. In 1908 he drove his brown mare, Dusky Dazzler in the class for horses over 15 hands and won an elegant cup that was offered by A. S. Bigelow. He often paired the two in tandem classes.[107]

Social Notes

On Friday, August 11, The *Boston Journal* notes, "Mrs. Plant Gives An Outing For Children. Twenty-five poor children from the North and West Ends were given an all day outing yesterday at the North Shore by Mrs. Thomas G. Plant of Jamaica Plain, one of many Boston women who are actively interested in settlement work. The children went to Magnolia by train, and from there were driven in a barge to North Manchester, where a spread was ready."

The Plants and Mrs. Griggs left the Masconomo that summer for the Charles Stedman Hanks' cottage in Manchester. This lovely property became their summer base for the next several summers. They are listed in the register "Who's Who Along the North Shore" for the summers 1908 and 1909.

Community Life

Tom's business acumen was admired. The leading issue for shoe manufacturers in the fall of 1905 was the escalating price of hides.[108] The National Shoe Manufacturers' Association advanced two approaches to deal with this pressing issue. First, they asked Tom to join a committee to urge President Roosevelt to reduce the tariff on hides. The second approach was to use newspapers to communicate with the shoe buying public, a tactic Tom had used earlier when dealing with his labor problems. It was decided to form a committee to raise $100,000 to fund a central bureau to manage an advertising campaign to educate the buying public why prices for shoes would need to be raised. Articles, written by the best writers of the day, would be placed in magazines and in large daily newspapers covering the entire United States and Canada in hopes that they would lend support to the Association's effort to seek a change in the tariff.[109]

His expertise was sought by the business community, and as a result he was asked to become a director of the International Trust Company in Boston and the Massachusetts Insurance League.[110] He was also invited to join the Advisory Committee for Boston's new High Commerce Institute, a high school to train students for a career in business.[111] He was elected to membership of the Merchants Club of Boston and asked to join the Boston Real Estate Exchange.[112] Tom's social and business affiliations were listed in Clark's Boston Blue Book in 1909. He was a member of the Metropolitan Improvement League working on the committee for the rearrangement of Copley Square. He was a member of the Boston Athletic Association, the Algonquin Club, the Massachusetts Savings Insurance League and a member of good standing in both the Metropolitan Driving Club and the Gentlemen's Driving Club of Boston.

As a member of the Massachusetts Savings Insurance League, Tom joined a number of business leaders including three former governors of the state in supporting the legislative passage of an act which would allow a new type of life insurance to be sold in the savings banks. Steps were to be taken for each participating bank to establish an insurance trust which would be kept entirely separate from the ordinary savings trust of the institution. He voiced his enthusiasm for this financial vehicle, "I wish to express my sincere belief that you have started a movement which will become as national and as great a benefit to the people of the United States as are our savings banks."[113] Tom had been very interested in the financial well being of his employees when he started a profit sharing and a savings fund department in 1903 for the company.

Caroline Plant continued working for children's interests and sponsoring programs in the arts for their benefit. She was appointed to the Examining Committee of the Boston Public Library which made suggestions for improvements for the Library. She and Tom were stockholders in the Boston Opera Company and were subscribers for society musicales on the North Shore. Tom, too, was engaged in programs for children. Along with fellow members of the Massachusetts Automobile Club he participated in an outing for children from The Gwynne Home, The Little Wanderers' Home and the Children's Mission. One particular day's event started at the automobile clubhouse and from there to a specific home where he picked up his little passengers for a fun day at Hoosick-Whisic Pond, Milton, where a luncheon and an afternoon of games were planned for the children.[114]

The Plants' schedule remained the same during these few years and revolved around horse shows, travel, hunting and fishing trips in Maine and New Brunswick and their society patronage events.

Their annual horse event schedule was full. The winter saw sleighing on the Charles River Speedway. The early spring horse show in Asheville, North Carolina was followed by the mid-April Boston Horse Show. The annual events continued with the Brookline Country Club and Chestnut Hill Horse shows following the Boston show. In June 1907, the Plants travelled to London for the International Horse Show to support the Alfred Gwynne Vanderbilt's four-in-hand grey team which won the competition.[115] The Newport (Rhode Island) Horse Show in September and the Brockton Fair Show in October continued the season and in November, 1908 they attended the New York Horse Show.

Sporting competitions made up a majority of their social life and Caroline Plant found a new one. She entered the dog show world with a pair of chocolate Pomeranians in the summer of 1909. Those who had seen the two little ones were very enthusiastic and pronounced them one of, if not the best, pair of American breeds ever raised.[116] In fact, in the New England Kennel Club Show the next February, Little Lord Fauntleroy won not only the Puppy Dog class, but also the Novice class.[117]

Shoe Machinery War

A project of great importance to shoe manufacturers all over the world began in the spring of 1906.

Boston Herald

"Boston, March 9, 1906 - A deal which may revolutionize the shoe machinery manufacturing industry and be of great importance to shoe manufacturers all over the world is about to be put through with Lynn as headquarters. Thomas G. Plant and other large capitalists are alleged to be behind the project.

"The scheme is the formation of a great corporation to fight the United Shoe Machinery Company, which has large factories at Beverly and other places, and agencies all over the country. It is said to be the largest shoe machinery manufacturing company in the world and also the only one in the world that manufactures all the different kinds of really up-to-date shoe machinery. The rule of the company is that factories using their machines must use them exclusively, so long as they are as satisfactory as those manufactured by any other company. If a company has some specialty which the United Shoe Machinery Company has not, manufacturers can use it, but, as matters stand, machines of the United Shoe Machinery Company are used almost entirely in the shoe industry.

"As a rule, the United Shoe Machinery people do not sell their machines. They will sell them outright or lease them. Prices are so arranged that it is cheaper to lease them. Consequently nearly every shoe manufacturer pays the United Shoe Machinery Company royalties, and only a few own their machines."[118]

More news was added in a *Boston Herald* article also published on March 9th —

Boston Herald

"Boston, March 9, 1906 - According to statements confidently made in Lynn yesterday, Mr. Plant has recently separated himself from all his stock in the Thomas G. Plant Company, and has been leasing shoe manufacturing machines from specialty manufacturers all over the country, with the idea of finally collecting enough machines to make up the complete outfit of up-to-date machinery needed to manufacture an entire shoe." The plan was to break the monopoly United had over its customers.

Although the news of his separation of his stock in the company was denied by friends, there was speculation that this new company was backed by New York capitalists including the Vanderbilts and English capitalists.[119]

The Bresnahan Shoe Machinery Company of Lynn which manufactures high-class speciality machinery was thought to be the nucleus of the new corporation.[120]

As the Shoe Machinery Trust War began, the Massachusetts Legislature tried to pass legislation that would be fair to United Shoe as the lessor and the shoe manufacturing companies, the lessees. From his point of view, Mr. Cassidy, a legislator from Berkshire, agreed that "The manufacturers of the state should be given all protection possible. He thought it a strange coincidence, though, that all bills aimed to curb the power of great corporations are at once attacked as unconstitutional. He maintained that the bill has been drawn to avoid objections on that ground. The state has the right to pass any law for the general social and commercial health of the state. The bill gives the shoe machinery company ample contract power, but restricts them in certain directions as against the public interest. He quoted from their present contracts to show their complete control of the business of the manufacturers. The prices charged for machinery repairs more than cover all expenses, although it is claimed they are made free. Furthermore, the United Shoe contracts required all materials needed to complete the manufacture of a shoe; needles, eyelets, and thread must be purchased from the company."[121]

A description of the shoe leases was distilled in a court case in March 1917, United States vs. United Shoe Machinery of New Jersey. "For the seventeen years term to which all the leases are drawn, the lessees upon failure to use exclusively the defendant's machines for lasting shoes, or upon failure to purchase needed additional machines from the lessor, or to buy certain supplies from the lessor at prices to be fixed by it, are subject to the right of the lessor to terminate all the leases held by the offending lessee and to take possession of the machines to the utter destruction of the lessee's business. The necessary effect of these prohibitive provisions, in view of the dominating control of the business by the lessor, is to prevent the lessee from using other similar machines however advantageous to him it may be to do so, unless he is willing to incur the peril of losing machinery essential to his business. It likewise so curtails the field of free customers as to keep others from manufacturing such machinery. Whenever a new machine is acquired by the lessee for the period of seventeen years (the full life of a patent under the statutes of the United States) the chain is forged anew which binds him to the use of the lessor's machines, to the practical exclusion of all others." This was the onerous "TYING CLAUSE" that resulted in making this practice a monopoly.

Breaking the monopoly in the shoe manufacturing machinery business proved to be difficult to do. There were some who felt shoes were priced higher because of the extensive fees and royalties charged by United. Some legislators felt altering the United's business plan jeopardized a company with a $2,000,000 payroll primarily in Massachusetts. While still others felt United's hold on the shoe machinery business stifled the creative genius needed to develop new and better machinery for the shoe industry.

Finally, the shoe machinery bill was passed. It required some modifications to the lease agreements with the shoe manufacturers that would be made in the future, but would not alter current lease agreements. However, an additional clause added to the new leases contained the following: "Independently of and in addition to all other rights hereunder the lessor shall have the right to terminate this lease and license at anytime upon 30 days' notice in writing to the lessee."[122] Advocates of the bill insisted it was constitutional and would put an end to the monopoly United Shoe currently enjoyed. Governor Guild signed the bill June 1, 1907. Opponents saw the clause as a threat that United could remove all the leased machinery with a 30 day notice and effectively close down a business.

The Bresnahan Shoe Machinery company in Lynn, working with Tom's backing to perfect a new line of shoe machinery, was developing new machinery that was not only going to surpass the machinery supplied by United Shoe, but was also going to revolutionize the manufacture of shoes. Maurice V. Bresnahan had long been a prominent figure in the shoe machinery world. He was a skilled machinist who refused to join the United Shoe Machinery Trust when it was formed in 1899. He explained "I didn't want to fight the United Shoe, they fought me. All I wanted was to be allowed to make and sell my own shoe machinery." Most of his legal battles were over patent rights and in most of them, Mr. Bresnahan won. It was one thing to manufacture machines, but another to sell them. Few wished to incur the hostility of United Shoe.[123]

Over the next few years over 120 patents were granted to Tom Plant for machinery developed by the Bresnahan, the C. P. Stanborn companies, both of Lynn, and the National Machinery Companies of South Boston.[124]

Rumors were everywhere. Questions about how many millions Plant had invested. Were the inventions superior enough to make the United machinery look primitive or were the Plant machines an entire failure and only good for junk? Plant wasn't talking and didn't even admit that he had the slightest interest in shoe machinery. But, one of his shoe machinery employees divulged to a *Boston Herald* reporter when asked if Mr. Plant was going to fight the United, "He isn't going to **try to** fight" was the emphatic reply. "He's **going to**."[125]

In 1907, after more than five years of peaceful working conditions, Tom Plant must have been very angered when he learned two of his trimming cutters were leading a movement to organize the employees. This was, of course, a breach of the signed agreement each employee made with the company beginning in 1901. Tom sent for the two cutters, told them he did not want a union and then discharged them. When they returned to their department and announced they'd been discharged, about 160 employees in the cutting department left in sympathy and were also discharged. Tom Plant was firm that he'd never run his factory other than as an "open shop."[126]

At the same time, the Thomas G. Plant Shoe Company factory continued to expand and a private and secure office was built on the roof of the company under Tom's instruction where he was able to manage both of his businesses, the shoe business and the shoe machinery business. There was a direct private elevator that accessed only this suite of rooms. Here he was surrounded by the same luxury that could be found in the most expensive hotel. It had been elegantly fitted for the president of the firm. The bathroom was marble with marble urinal, marble fixtures and brass faucets.[127] The suite also had a bedroom and a larger office space where private meetings could be held. Meetings with his shoe machinery developers could be totally secure and the progress in perfecting his complete set of shoe machinery could be held totally under wraps.[128] It was here in this office that a final agreement to settle the long-running dispute with the United Shoe Machinery Company was finally made.[129]

In the midst of the legal battle with the United Shoe Machinery company, Tom Plant was said to display the energy of three healthy men. It was also known that during this legal fight he was constantly attended by physicians and trained masseurs who worked over him at the end of each business day.

THE THOMAS G. PLANT COMPANY.

Tom Plant's office on the roof of the Thomas G. Plant Shoe Company

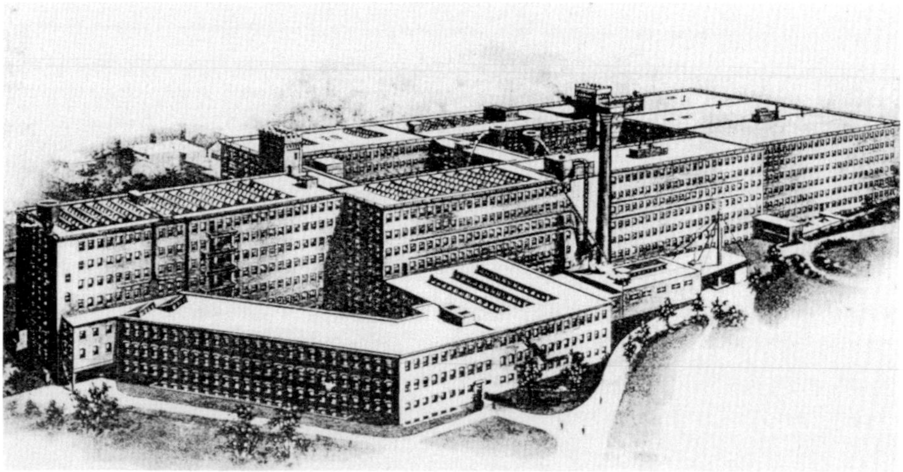

1910 — A Crucial Year

The large bold headline in the January 6, 1910 *Boston Herald* announced —

PLANT PLANS SHOE

MACHINERY WAR

Is Putting Into Jamaica Plain

Factory Complete Equipment,

The Patents for Which He

Owns or Controls

This wasn't a surprise to shoe manufacturers, nor was it a surprise to United Shoe Machinery Company. They'd known since March 1906 that Tom Plant had thrown down the gauntlet and was preparing to enter the shoe machinery business. They could watch the listings as Tom registered and acquired patents either in his name or the name of an inventor who assigned them to Tom. They could only wonder about the efficiency of his inventions as the machinery developed was shrouded in secrecy. To guard their design, individual pieces of equipment were fabricated in different machine shops he controlled throughout the state and were assembled in his factory under strict security. Furthermore, there were two new factory buildings constructed, each 50 x 200 feet, expressly for the new machinery.

There was speculation that he'd spent millions of his own money and that he was backed by large corporations and large shoe manufacturers who wished to save themselves millions in licensing fees and royalties. It's possible to believe the American Consolidated Shoe Machinery business that was established in 1901 had a vested interest also. A major concern for potential buyers was the certainty that patent suits would be brought by United Shoe. Could the battle be won? Tom Plant's development of a complete line of shoe machinery that could produce an entire shoe was a substantial threat to United, but United Shoe was very strong financially and had the ability to spend millions to protect its patents and exclusive leases.

Although Tom had divorced himself from his own stock in his shoe company in 1906, the leases that had been signed with United Shoe remained an obligation of Tom Plant and the Thomas G. Plant Shoe Company. He had broken his lease agreements with United Shoe by removing its machinery and installing his own Wonder Worker machines.[130] If he were able to break his lease with United Shoe and use the Wonder Worker machinery he would save a reported $100,000 annually in royalties. However, his plan was to not only use these machines in his own factory, but primarily to sell them to other shoe manufacturers. His new machines were faster and more automatic than the leased machinery. They had the advantage that they didn't require as much training to operate and production rates could be increased.

By June, an announcement was issued to shoe manufacturers regarding his Wonder Worker Shoe Machinery Company. His statement accompanied a descriptive circular of his advancements in improving modern shoe machinery and methods of manufacture.

"Six years ago I first undertook to investigate the patents and new leases of the United Shoe Machinery Company, and, after securing all necessary information, proceeded to devote time and money in developing a line of shoe machinery that will not only save the shoe trade millions of dollars in royalties now paid to the shoe machinery trust, but will save millions of dollars per annum by economies in the use of materials and labor and at the same time greatly improve the quality of shoemaking.

"In connection with this write-up of the Wonder Worker Shoe Machinery Company, I am inclosing also a descriptive write-up of the Thomas G. Plant Company's establishment, which exemplifies the possibilities of advancement in shoe making by the use of modern shoe machinery and methods.

"The advantage the Thomas G. Plant Company possesses in the use of the Wonder Worker non-royalty machinery cannot but bring forcibly to the mind of the progressive shoe manufacturer the advantages he, too, may have by equipping his factory with like machinery.

"Our whole aim has been to assist the operators, keeping constantly before us the difficulty in obtaining skilled workmen in sufficient numbers. We did not alone consider high speed machines essential, but in order that the operators might readily do good work, we did consider it essential that the machines be, so far as possible, automatic, leaving to the operator the simple task of directing their operations.

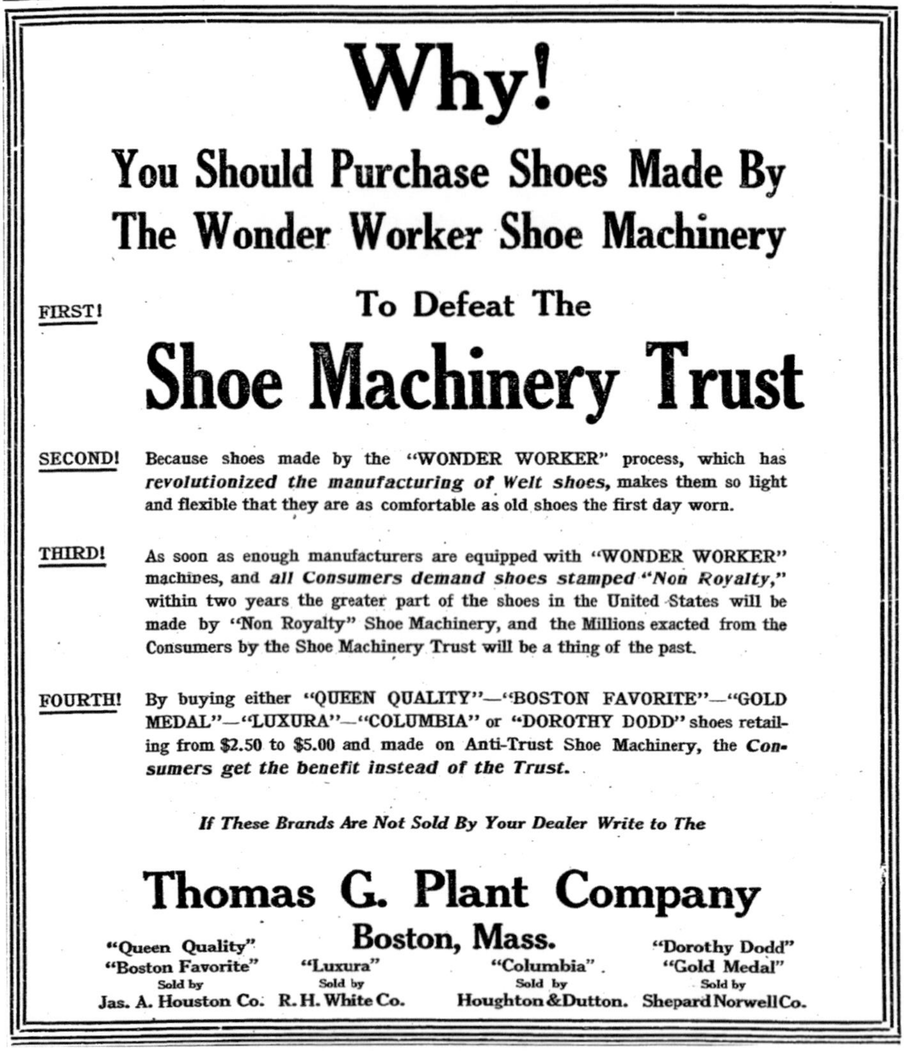

"To produce good work with the antiquated machines put out by the Shoe Machinery Trust absolutely requires skilled workmen. Our machines solve the great problem of today, viz., to improve the quality of fine shoe making at the lowest possible cost. We also can enable the makers of medium priced shoes to turn out work equal to that heretofore produced only by makers of fine shoes."[131]

Once again, Tom Plant used the newspapers to tell his story to the consumer.[132]

There was a natural hesitancy on the part of shoe manufacturers to risk the patent suits that United Shoe was sure to bring against them. Plant's answer was to inform potential buyers that he would provide indemnification as witnessed in his statement — "To meet the objection that a manufacturer accepting the Plant machines is certain to be subject to patent suits and injunctions brought by the United Shoe, Mr. Plant will furnish a bond to each purchaser indemnifying him against loss and, where possible, substituting himself as a party to the suit."[133]

There was also the uncertainty about the cost of maintaining the Wonder Worker machinery. If the manufacturers were to remain with United, would the convenience, although costly, of having United keep their leased machines in good repair and replacing them when necessary, be worth it?

By early July, Tom had placed an article entitled "FACTS ABOUT THE SITUATION IN SHOE MACHINERY" in several newspapers. The article was three columns wide above and below the fold and was signed at the bottom, THOMAS G. PLANT. This was a broad brush appeal to shoe manufacturers and consumers alike to explain the United leases and another option, his Wonder Worker Machinery. This is some of what he wrote:

"The manufacturers who have examined the machines, without exception or reservation, have pronounced the Wonder Worker Machinery superior in every respect to the machines of the United Company.

"Two of the foremost lawyers of Boston, employed separately by different manufacturers, acting solely in their interest and in no way retained by or connected with the Plant interests, have given the opinion that the 'Leases' of the United Company are in violation of law, void, and of no binding effect; that, therefore, the manufacturers are at liberty to return the United machines and install the new Wonder Worker Machinery.

"For further assurance, Messrs. Gifford & Bull of New York City, leading patent attorneys of the United States, after careful examination have given an opinion that the Wonder Worker machines in no way infringe the United Company's patents or any of them."[134]

The next day, July 8, United Shoe Machinery answered back, "The United Shoe Machinery Company is quite vexed at Thomas G. Plant and the Thomas G. Plant Company, and filed a bill in the (State)

Supreme Court yesterday asking they be enjoined from using independent machines of certain kinds when the leased Shoe Machinery machines are not running up to their full capacity."[135] Their bill stated that Plant stopped using United Shoe Machinery in April and since then has only partially complied with the terms of his lease agreements.

Plant countered that the agreement between the United Company and the manufacturers was illegal. When he asked the United Company to remove its machines last winter in order to put in a set of his machines, they refused to do so. The Plant Company took out the machines and stored them.[136]

IS THE UNITED SHOE MACHINERY COMPANY AN ILLEGAL TRUST AND MONOPOLY?

ARE ITS SO CALLED LEASES VALID AND BINDING, OR ILLEGAL AND UNENFORCEABLE?

EMINENT LAWYERS WHO HAVE EXAMINED THE SUBJECT HAVE GIVEN OPINIONS ON THESE QUESTIONS.

Boston Journal, Friday, July 8, 1910, Page:12

The law firm of Gaston, Snow & Saltonstall of Boston answered; "Their opinion is the contracts of the United Shoe Machinery Company are in violation of the Sherman Act, so-called; that they are illegal and void, and that if you choose to give up the shoe machinery which you hold under them no action can be successfully maintained against you by reason thereof." Sherman L. Wipple, Esq., added, "The United Company, as organized, is itself a combination in restraint of trade, existing in violation of law. Additionally the leases themselves tend to restrain and monopolize trade and commerce."[137]

Has the United Shoe Machinery Company in Reality the Boasted Patent Monopoly Which It Claims?

Boston Journal, Friday, July 8, 1910, Page:12

A number of prominent patent attorneys answered this question emphatically. Frederick L. Emery, Esq., of Messrs. Emery, Booth, Janney & Varney, Patent Attorneys stated "In my opinion Mr. Plant's machines embody designs and methods in shoe making so far advanced beyond existing methods as to render the patents of the United Company largely obsolete and ineffective." The opinion of Livingston Gifford, Esq., of

Gifford & Bull, Patent Counsel, New York City concurred, as did Robert P. Hains, Esq., formerly Principal Examiner United States Patent Office.

Charles H. Jones, President of The Commonwealth Shoe & Leather Co. wrote to Tom Plant after examining the Wonder Worker Machines in the Plant Shoe factory, "We can say with fullest conviction that you have shown us machinery that will make our grades of welt shoes better, and more uniform in quality and appearance, than any machinery that we have ever seen or used before."[138] Another prominent shoe manufacturer, Henry B. Endicott, a friend of Tom's, also made a public endorsement of the new shoe machinery installed in the Plant factory.[139] Endicott was to have a prominent role as a liaison between Tom Plant and Sidney Winslow of United Shoe Machinery Company. Winslow formalized Endicott's relationship with his company by inviting him onto the Board of Directors.

As expected, United Shoe filed a bill in the United States Circuit Court on Friday, July 29 personally against both Thomas G. Plant and the Thomas G. Plant Shoe Company for not making payments for the leases of shoe machinery for April and May of this year as well as patent infringement on several patents held by United Shoe Machinery Co. "Thomas G. Plant was further alleged to have willfully induced the Thomas G. Plant Shoe Co. to violate its leases with the plaintiff, and asked to be enjoined from furnishing further machines."[140]

The pleas filed by Thomas G. Plant and the Thomas G. Plant Shoe Co. were essentially the same; "It is declared that the United Shoe Machinery Company is a combination of competing shoe machinery companies, in violation of the Sherman anti-trust act, and that leases it gives are used to assist it in maintaining its monopoly and are, therefore invalid. The Plant Company complains that the leases prevent it from getting machinery of a superior efficiency which will enable it to manufacture better shoes for the public, at the same price, while Plant's personal plea complains that he is shut out from the shoe machinery business by the monopoly of the plaintiff."[141]

Legal skirmishing in the courts continued into September. In the meantime, an announcement of the filed articles of incorporation of the Wonder Worker Shoe Machinery Co., in Montclair, NJ, with a capitalization of $10,000,000, appeared in the Boot and Shoe Recorder on September 19, 1910. "The company is organized to manufacture, operate, purchase, sell, lease, and deal in all sorts of foot, shoe and footwear machinery, lasts, trees, forms, and supplies."[142]

Tom Plant had "a reputation throughout the shoe world as a hard-headed business man and also as a 'game one.' "[143] Everyone was watching. Every shoe manufacturer paid United Shoe a royalty on every shoe manufactured and they were giving Tom their moral support to win the fight.

By September 23, it was obvious something had happened when 350 men who worked in the Bresnahan factory and the 150 employees in the Charles P. Stanbon Company owned by Tom Plant were laid off. What was going on? Had a settlement been made?

The *Boston Financial News* issued a report that a gentlemen's agreement between the United Shoe Machinery and Tom Plant had been reached. It continued that the first offer was $5,000,000 but speculated that the figure could be as high as the $10,000,000 capitalization.

The *Boot and Shoe Recorder*, in the September 28 issue reported that "the settlement of differences between the United Shoe Machinery Company and Thomas G. Plant has been in progress for the past week. President Sidney W. Winslow and his shoe machinery experts have visited the Plant factory at Jamaica Plain and in company with Mr. Plant and Director H. B. Endicott have carefully studied the workings of the Wonder Worker machines. It is understood that Mr. Winslow became convinced that the Plant machines could do satisfactory work and that a purchase was warranted at Mr. Plant's price."

Three issues determined the timing of the settlement between Plant and United. The first was that the United States Circuit Court was going to hear arguments from Sherman L. Whipple who represented Plant on the monopoly and restraint-of-trade issues.[144] The second was that Plant had financial obligations due October 1, but found his credit had been inexplicably cut off. The third was the arrival in Boston of shoe manufacturers from the West representing twenty-five per cent of the shoe industry in the United States who came prepared to offer Mr. Plant unlimited credit for the manufacture and installations of his machines. They were eager to do so because a complete set of superior Wonder Worker machines that could completely equip a factory would make them independent from the United Shoe Machinery Company. Plant met with this group but the Western Alliance could not agree among themselves on terms quickly enough. Unfortunately, their offer came too late to help Plant, but the Alliance continued their efforts to fight United.

During this period of uncertainty in the shoe world, the questions about Tom Plant's credit, the price he realized for his machinery and shoe business interests and the size of his net worth were the subject of endless speculation. Some of the answers were obtained in court settlements and legal hearings.

A *Boston Herald* article on September 28, 1910 summed up the reason Tom Plant made the deal to sell out to United Shoe. "A year ago he began placing his paper with a New York firm of note brokers. These brokers always found a sale for his paper, and were ready when a note came due to renew it on terms satisfactory to Mr. Plant.

"There was never any difficulty in meeting Mr. Plant's growing requirements. He had only to ask for a loan and the money was forthcoming, without regard to the general condition of the money market. Others might be having difficulty in placing their paper, but Mr. Plant's note brokers never intimated to him that money was scarce.

"Mr. Plant had obligations amounting to $1,500,000 coming due Oct. 1, next Saturday. He anticipated no difficulty in renewing these, for his collateral had not deteriorated; in fact, it was reasonable to assume that the collateral was increasing in value every day.

"A fortnight ago he was astounded - as his friends tell the story — to get word that his notes would not be renewed. He went to New York to get an explanation of this abrupt change in the attitude of his brokers. They told him, without any dissembling, that they had been selling his notes to the United Shoe Machinery Company.

"That was quite enough for Mr. Plant. He had the alternative of raising a million and a half in a few days or making peace with his bitter foe." The best option for both Plant and United was to reach an agreement. So he came back to Boston, and met with President Winslow of the United Shoe Company, whom he disliked, and Henry B. Endicott, whom he trusted. "The stock of United Shoe rose in value the next day."[145]

The agreement to sell his properties was made September 22 with a payment of $1,000,000. "Under the conditions of the transfer Mr. Plant received $3,000,000 in cash and $3,000,000 in stock of the United Shoe Machinery Company."[146] A separate agreement was made with Plant for his interest in the Bresnahan, Stanley and Sanborn machinery companies.[147]

On Saturday, September 24, the *Boston Financial News* clarified, "We can state that Mr. Plant was not embarrassed financially and was not forced to sell, but that he was willing to sell part or all of his business after his advertising campaign last June, is conceded. He made offers to shoe manufacturers, but kept available an opportunity to sell to the United Shoe Machinery Corporation. Both of these possibilities for sale were open until the time at which the trade was finally made, which was at a conference beginning at 6 o'clock on the evening of Thursday, Sept. 22, and ended at 4 o'clock the next morning.

"Although Mr. Plant had large notes to meet on Oct. 1, he had plenty of resources to meet them, and we understand that he was not cramped in his finances. His entire financing of his shoe machinery business had been in his own name without the use of the Thomas G. Plant Company, which had not borrowed any money through brokers since last June."

On October 8, the *Bath Independent* weighed in: "The sale of the Wonder Worker machinery to the United Shoe Machinery Company, has made Thomas G. Plant a much talked of man in all parts of the country and nowhere more than in Boston where he has become a figure in the world of shoes and finance. Plant is reckoned as a level headed, cool and keen business man and it seems to be generally accepted that he knows pretty well what he is doing."

"Boston financiers as well as the *Boston News Letter* seem to believe that Plant benefitted himself by selling out and that he did it at just the right time, when he could get a good big price as well as relieve himself of additional care and worry. It is said that the fact that some St. Louis capitalists, whom the shoe machinery company may have feared, arrived in Boston just before the sale with the intention of buying and at that time the United company dropped in and bought quickly rather than take any chances of the patents and machines getting into more powerful hands."[148]

But lawsuits were on the horizon. "A verdict for $96,000, with $13,168 interest was returned by a jury in the Superior Court for James A. Hutchinson of Lynn in his $125,000 suit against Thomas G. Plant for his commission and expenses in soliciting $2,500,000 additional capital in 1910 for Plant's 'Wonder Worker' shoe machinery."[149] Tom admitted that there had been negotiations, but that the parties involved never reached an agreement so Hutchinson was not entitled to remuneration.

Retirement

Shoe industrialist no more. The development of a complete collection of the essential shoe machinery for the manufacture of women's shoes was a monumental achievement. The Thomas G. Plant Shoe Company had products that satisfied the market taste and his employees were content. This was a good time to retire. The end of such a successful business career must have given Tom Plant some pause. Along the way he had garnered a great deal of respect as an enlightened industrialist and at the same time made a fortune. It was estimated that he was worth $30,000,000, but there was no way to confirm that.

News of a gift to employees was confirmed by the office of the company with the added information that "Mr. Plant will, after the first of the year, cease to be a member of the firm." Over $100,000 in freshly minted gold coins were given to the employees with the letter that follows. It was confirmed that an additional gift of $50,000 would follow later next year under similar conditions.

Letter To Employees

Dec. 27, 1910

I believe length of service to a great extent expresses the individual's loyalty to his employer. The rapid growth and success of the Thomas G. Plant Company is undoubtedly due, in a great measure, to those having been in its employ four years or more, and in proportion to the years of employment and service they have rendered.

As I am retiring permanently from business, I desire to express my sincere appreciation of your loyal service, and as a partial expression of my good wishes have inclosed the sum of ——

Wishing you success and happiness for the future, I remain, very truly yours,

(Signed) Thomas G. Plant[150]

United Shoe Under Investigation

United Shoe thought that the purchase of Tom Plant's businesses would be the end of it. They were wrong! Two unexpected government probes into United Shoe were announced in 1911. The first announcement on July 26 came from United States District Attorney, Asa P. French and Special United States Assistant Attorney General, William S. Gregg, Assistant to United States Attorney General Wickersham. Gregg and French planned to present evidence they'd obtained in a probe of the United Company to a federal grand jury Tuesday, August 1, 1911. The *Boston Journal* in the July 27, 1911 paper began an article: "Believes United Shoe Co. is Guilty - Government Probe Results in Calling Grand Jury in Special Session. The United States government is convinced it has in its possession sufficient evidence to secure an indictment of the United Shoe Machinery Company for violating the Sherman anti-trust act by maintaining a monopoly in restraint of trade."

At the same time, Gov. Eugene Foss of Massachusetts pushed for a state investigation of United Shoe as well. He had been hearing complaints from Massachusetts shoe manufacturers who had been hampered by the same machinery lease agreements that Tom Plant had fought against. Foss pushed Massachusetts Attorney General Swift into conducting an investigation.[151]

It would be hard to believe Tom was unaware of the government probe into the United Shoe Machinery Company. "The Grand Jury sat for nearly a month considering the evidence presented by seventy-five witnesses who were brought to Boston by special agents of the Department of Justice at Washington from all parts of the country, but especially from New England."[152] Tom must have had some satisfaction when indictments were returned September 19 against both the officers of the company and the company itself for alleged violations of the Sherman Anti-Trust Act and conspiracy in restraint of trade.

The *Boston Herald*'s front page article on September 20, "James J. Storrow, Sidney W. Winslow, Edward P. Hurd, George W. Brown and Elmer P. Howe of Boston and William Barbour of New York were yesterday indicted by the United States circuit court grand jury on charges of having unlawfully engaged in a corrupt combination in undue, unreasonable and direct restraint of interstate business, trade and commerce, in connection with the United Shoe Machinery Company of Boston."[153]

In December 1911, a civil suit was filed by United States District Attorney French, acting under the direction of Attorney General Wickersham, to dissolve the United Shoe Machinery Company. Centered in Boston, the company was alleged to control 98% of the shoe machinery of the country and was capitalized at over $71,000,000. The petition also asked that lease and license agreements be declared void and the defendants refrain from making or enforcing these agreements. The two principal corporations, the United Shoe Machinery Company of New Jersey and the United Shoe Machinery Corporation were named along with 13 subsidiary corporations and 23 individuals, the majority of the latter, Massachusetts men.[154]

Louis D. Brandeis, a prominent Boston attorney who was to later become a United States Supreme Court Justice, spoke during deliberations about his reconsideration of the leases of the United Shoe Machinery Company. He had been placed on the board of directors at the company's origination in 1899 as the representative of a family who had a very large holding of the company's stock. He had approved the United leases and royalty system until 1906 when the Massachusetts legislature was working on legislation to protect the interests of the shoe manufacturers as well as the so-called "shoe machinery trust." He had felt that there were good trusts as well as bad trusts and that the company was managed by men in whose ability and judgment he had confidence. He began to understand the lease issue from the manufacturer's point of view and rather than take up the issue in opposition to the rest of the board, he quietly resigned.

As previously noted, in 1910 the United Shoe Machinery Company was confronted with a competitor so formidable that the company felt obligated to buy him out, though it was a violation of the law. "Thomas G. Plant, a shoe manufacturer who had resented the domination of the trust, developed an extensive system of shoe machinery, which is believed to be superior to the trust's own system, which represents the continuous development of the company and its predecessors for nearly half a century.

"H. B. Endicott, one of the leading shoe manufacturers of the country and now a director in the Shoe Machinery trust, publicly declared, after examining the Plant system, 'In my judgment and that of my experts, what you [Plant] has shown us was by far the most perfect set of working machinery that we have ever seen, or expected to see.' "[155]

By March 2, 1912 the court rejected four of the five indictments against the company's officials, but left the charge of a monopoly through the leases on patented machinery. United States District Attorney French indicated the two broad counts remaining would allow all the evidence which supported the rejected indictments would be admitted at the trial.[156] United Shoe appealed this decision and the case was sent to the Supreme Court.

In July 1912 there were efforts to reach a friendly settlement in the civil and criminal anti-trust suits against United Shoe by the Department of Justice. The following June 1913 a witness in the "threat" clause portion in the government's suit against United gave testimony which would be very familiar to Tom Plant. "The principal witness for the government was James N. Darragh of New York, formerly a director and chairman of the executive committee of the Standard Shoe Machinery Company which went into receivership in 1901. He testified that William Barbour of New York, a director of the United Company had told him, when he refused to sell out, that the United first tried to buy and then forced competitors out of business. Mr. Barbour had said, the witness testified, that he could not get any money to carry on his business because the influence of the United with the banks of New York and Boston was so great."[157]

Antitrust litigation into United Shoe's leasing practices continued for decades until 1968 when the Supreme Court interpreted the Sherman Act to find that the United Shoe Machinery Corporation had engaged in monopolist practices and ordered USM to be broken up.[158]

DIFFICULT TIMES

Tom and Caroline Plant 1910

1910 Estrangement

We could surmise that the amount of time and energy Tom was devoting to his machinery business and the frequency of his absence from home would cause some tension in his marriage. But, it was actually Caroline's discovery of a bank statement with the name Catherine Haberley on it that precipitated a confrontation between Tom and Caroline. This was around September 10. Mrs. Plant said: "On hearing of his relations with the girl, I took him to task for it. He declared he was simply interested in her and wanted to give her an education, and that there was nothing wrong in their relations." He moved out of their suite in the Somerset and arranged another suite in the hotel for himself.[159] They saw each other every day in the dining hall and corridors of the hotel, but never spoke.

From September on, Caroline Plant worked tirelessly and secretly finding out who Catherine Haberley was and investigating the relationship. She traveled hundreds of miles in her investigations tracking their travels. She found that Catherine had worked at the shoe plant as a waitress and had met Tom there. She was known as "Kitty Hadley" a quiet young

Englishwoman who had been serving Tom his meals in his private dining room for the last few months. In February, 1911, friends of Kitty Hadley, the Joseph Greeman family of Jamaica Plain, said she had lived with them for eight years, first as household help and then boarding with them after she had begun work at the shoe factory. They included her in their 1900 Census form: "Kate Hadley, servant, birth September 1882, 17 years old, born in England, emigrated in 1896." The Greemans said she was a quiet girl who spent her evenings at home unless she was visiting one of the neighbors. Since she'd left Boston in the summer of 1910, she had returned once and was tastefully, but simply dressed. She had found work as a lady's maid in New York City.[160]

The Sporting Life Continues

However, both Tom and Caroline continued separately showing their horses at the same events throughout the fall. They entered the usual classes at the Boston Horse Show, Chestnut Hill, Reading-Wakefield and Brockton Fairs, and the Metropolitan Driving Club's Show at the Charles River Speedway. Close friends knew something was in the air and had noticed a change in their relationship, so their direct competition in the same class must have been watched with interest. The headline —

Mrs. Thomas G. Plant's Sunlight Gets Blue Ribbon in Runabout Class

at the Whitney Horse Show at Meadowbrook must have interested friends. Thomas Plant came in second with Cherry Boy.[161]

1911 Lawsuits

Late January 1911, the headline that was emblazoned on newspapers across the country from Bellingham, Washington to Winston-Salem, North Carolina to New York City surprised few who knew them; "Thomas G. Plant Sued by Wife." One specific of the suit for libel was an attachment of Mr. Plant's property for $1,500,000 by the court. That figure was eye opening! [162]

At the same time that Caroline was suing Tom, Harry W. Smith sued Tom Plant for $400,000, which he claimed was due him for "effecting the transfer of the Wonder Worker machine Company to the United Shoe Machinery Company." He maintained that Mr. Plant offered him a 5% commission if he were instrumental in bringing about the transaction with United Shoe for the sale of his company. Smith had introduced Tom to Col. William Barbour of New York and Robert F. Herrick of Boston, both members of the Board of Directors of the United Shoe Machinery Company.[163] An additional attachment amounting to $400,000 was made on Plant's bank accounts and real estate bringing the total to $1,900,000. Constables arrived at the Hotel Somerset and served Tom with the papers for both suits. Tom left Boston immediately on the next train to New York where he maintained a suite in the Hotel Gotham.

A *Boston Journal* article noted "While the attachment is the largest in the history of the Suffolk County Court it will not in any way affect Mr. Plant's bank account. He is credited with over $30,000,000 deposits and real estate."[164]

Tom Plant's testimony in the Smith case was interesting; he held three-fifths of the stock in his shoe company that was capitalized for $3,750,000, a profitable business that payed large dividends. He had 680 patents and 70 machines of his own design and had expended $3,600,000 in perfecting the machinery and obtaining patents which he controlled. In 1913, a jury award of $323,750 ($300,000 plus interest) in favor of Harry W. Smith of Worchester was returned in the Superior Court against Thomas G. Plant of Boston.[165] Tom planned to appeal the verdict.

In her court suit, Caroline claimed her husband had been unfaithful to her in Bangor and Calais, Maine during October 1909 as well as St. George, New Brunswick and New York on other occasions. This promised to be an interesting case.

According to the *New York Times*, "Their marriage up to about a year ago had been considered a happy one. The couple was constantly seen at society entertainments, especially horse shows and country club meets. Mr. Plant owned a number of fine horses, and his wife showed them to advantage by exhibiting them, both in harness and under saddle, at the various meets all over New England."[166]

Good News Among The Bad

Better news had come a couple of days earlier — On January 18, 1911 United Shoe Machinery Company dropped all suits against Thomas Plant for patent infringement. The suits had been pending in the United States District Court. Judge Lowell dismissed the case without prejudice and without costs since United now held the patents on Plant's shoe machinery.[167]

More good news arrived. In January the engagement of Tom's niece, Amy Elizabeth Plant, William and Margaret Plant's daughter, was announced and a tea was held in her honor. She was to marry Edward Denning Van Tassel in October 1912.[168]

Divergent Lives

The Plants were leading separate lives. The *Boston Herald* issue on Sunday, August 6, 1911 had an article on page 2 about the Cohasset Horse Show where Mrs. Thomas G. Plant would "seek blue ribbons" and on page 5, an article describing the riot on Thomas G. Plant's estate in Moultonborough, New Hampshire.

Speculation about the Plants' divorce case arose in mid summer when its continued absence from the Court calendar led to the belief that there might have been a reconciliation. However, both Tom and Caroline were busy in separate endeavors - she with her interests in her horses and now dogs and he with planning his summer home. Then in the fall she began to discharge some of the attachments on his funds even though the divorce case was still pending in the court. By November 10, she had released attachments for the fifth time.[169] Interest surged. More curiosity as all of this was covered by the press.

By November, Caroline and her mother made a decision. At the age of 89, her mother, Mary Jane Griggs, purchased two parcels of contiguous land forming a property of about 28 acres. It had been the home of Anna L. P. Williams, widow of Alexander Williams. The property was on the east side of S. Main Street in Cohasset, Massachusetts. The deed was recorded with the Norfolk Registry of Deeds, Book 1196, page 246. On June 19, 1912, Mrs. Griggs transferred the deed to Caroline G. Plant. It was recorded in the Norfolk Deeds Book 1247, page 89. This was to be their summer home.[170] "Beechwood" was the name of the Alexander Williams estate, Caroline renamed it "Riverview."

Caroline began making alterations to her new property early in the spring of 1912. Interest in her marital situation piqued when it was reported she was seeing Tom and the newspapers speculated that the couple had reconciled. She was said to have "admitted that on two occasions she had met her husband by 'the merest accident' and that their exchange of greetings was cordial."[171] Further pressed, "Mr. Plant has visited me at my summer home in Cohasset," Mrs. Plant said…"that is all I care to say."[172]

Hoping to quell further interest in a supposed reconciliation, Mrs. Plant consented to a lengthy interview with the *Boston Sunday Post* on June 16, 1912.

"While Mrs. Plant has been having her summer estate renovated she has been staying at the Woodland Park Hotel at Auburndale and it was there that a *Sunday Post* reporter chatted with her. She had just returned from a reception. She was gowned in a pink satin creation that set off most beautifully her iron gray hair and clear blue eyes. The low cut gown revealed a perfect neck from whose pearly whiteness sparkled a perfect diamond. Around her neck was clasped a band of black velvet on which were pinned diamonds ranging from small to large. Her hands, and they were strong hands, too, were ornamented by simple yet perfect stones.

"But with all her diamonds and her pink satin gown she did not resemble a woman of the idle rich. There was that indefinable something that marked her as a woman with a purpose, a woman who would walk miles for what she wished, a woman who would never forget a kindness. If she had been gowned in a tailor-made waist and skirt one would describe her as a thorough business woman.

"Sitting in the blue drawing room of the hotel she was a living proof that a woman is not at her best when sweet 16. She had the look of the matron who could procure partners for the dance, when the wallflowers were numbered in the dozens.

" 'How are you passing the time now-days?' Was the first question asked Mrs. Plant.

" 'I don't have to pass the time. The time just seems to dance by me without even hesitating,' she exclaimed.

" 'Is there to be a reconciliation between you and Mr. Plant?' was asked.

"Her sparkling blue eyes seemed to snap fire and the mouth formed into the straightest of lines as she answered, 'Reconciliation! There will never be a reconciliation. The stories circulated about that are mere fairy tales.'

“ ‘It has been said that Mr. Plant came to Cohasset. This is untrue. I have never talked to a reporter before in my life, but I will say now that Mr. Plant has absolutely nothing to do with Cohasset. He has his place and I have mine.’

“ ‘We are far apart, you see, and this reconciliation talk is very tiring to me. I am going to spend my summer at my home at Cohasset which I am having all changed about. I have six Pomeranians and with them and my horses, for which I am having a tan bark track built, I shall enjoy the summer.’

“ ‘I am going to try to forget my worries. It is very lucky for me that I love animals, for the person who loves dogs can always say she has company. A dog is always a friend. He will remain by one’s side when everybody else has turned away.’

“ ‘My position in the divorce suit has not been a pleasant one. It is not very enviable. I can assure you, and the fact that I have my summer home where I can have my pets gives me something to look forward to.’

“ ‘It takes a woman who has been through what I have been to really understand. A woman who has never had such trouble cannot understand the situation any more than a child. It makes me very unhappy when I think of it, for I cannot imagine anything worse than suing for divorce. Perhaps people might care to hear just what the conclusions of the case have been, but I can’t tell because of private reasons. I can say, however, that a reconciliation is not to take place.’ ”[173]

Complicating this story were contemporary news reports that Tom had paid for some improvements at Riverview by workmen who said he’d written checks for thousands of dollars. One explanation may be the complicated financial arrangement of Caroline’s libel suit. No information about her release of some of his funds had been given. An interesting story also became part of the libel suit. Tom was said to have placed a check in her napkin ring for $1,000,000. This story was later verified by family.[174]

Rumors of reconciliation ended completely with the headline: **“PLANT DIVORCE WILL BE TRIED.”** “Mrs. Thomas G. Plant’s divorce libel against her husband, the Jamaica Plain shoe manufacturer, will be tried during the October divorce session, which opens Monday. It is on the uncontested list.”[175] The hearing included the testimony of several witnesses. John McGerr of St. George, N.B. identified Tom Plant as traveling with an unknown veiled woman whom he knew was not Mrs. Plant. Florence Stoddard, a teacher and journalist of Brooklyn, New York testified that she had "answered an advertisement in a New York paper which sought a lady of refinement and education who would undertake to educate a lady whose education had been neglected." She arranged to meet Plant at the Murray Hill Hotel where he had a private suite. He explained to Mrs. Stoddard that his "niece" had had no advantages and "he wanted to educate his niece so she might travel pleasantly and might appear in cultured society."[176] In early September, 1909, Catherine went to Brooklyn to live with Mrs. Stoddard. First introduced as Miss Hadley, Plant corrected the name to Haberley. The theatre, opera and horseback riding lessons were all part of the program to broaden the horizons of this young woman and a trip abroad was being planned. There was daily correspondence between Tom and Catherine. One discarded letter, found by Mrs. Stoddard, revealed their relationship. Stoddard immediately confronted Plant about being misled. After this meeting, Catherine moved back to the Murray Hill Hotel and her relationship with Florence Stoddard ended. Several years later travel documents revealed that she was living at 371 Central Park West in New York City, perhaps as a lady's maid.[177] It has never been disclosed how her relationship with Tom Plant ended.

"MRS. T. G. PLANT GETS DIVORCE" This was the headline in the October 29, 1912 *Boston Journal*. "The Suffolk Divorce Court Judge Hardy granted a Decree Nisi to Mrs. Caroline G. Plant, without alimony, after hearing five witnesses." In Massachusetts, there is a waiting period of 90 days before a divorce is absolute. In November, Caroline Plant moved to a suite at the Plaza Hotel, Fifth Avenue, New York City. "New York's two long-established society turnouts, the horse and dog shows, will probably find her a prominent figure in the gathering of wealth owners this winter. She is a great lover of horses and an excellent horsewoman. She has some valuable Pomeranian dogs."[178]

Caroline Plant moved on with her life and her interests. She owned magnificent gardens on her estate at Cohasset, Massachusetts which were designed by Olmstead Brothers.[179] Her philanthropy was well known - if it were a benefit, her purse was always open and her home and gardens, too. In 1938, she engaged James Gamble Rogers, II to design a home for her in Winter Park, Florida, "Merrywood." "At nearly 7,000 square feet, it's the largest residence ever designed by Rogers. When Caroline died in 1947, the house was sold and her estate was distributed to Rollins College and other charitable organizations."[180]

She also left instructions in her will to have all the contents of her homes, including personal items sold and additionally left $150,000 to the needy in both Cohasset, Massachusetts and Winter Park, Florida. She left an additional amount for the victims of unusual disasters, such as hurricanes, explosions or conflagrations.[181]

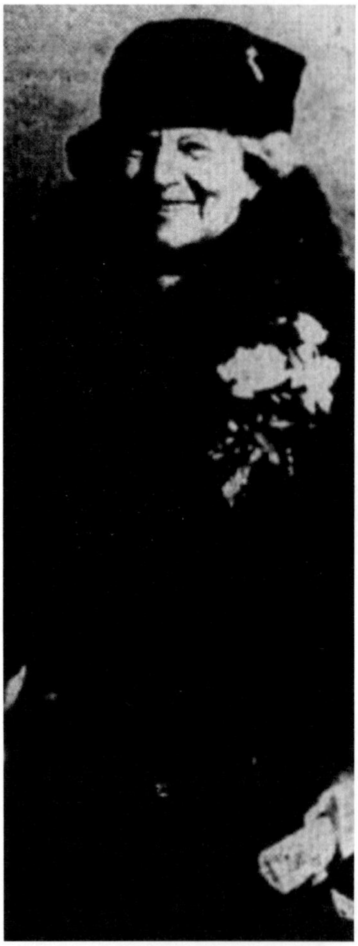

Caroline Griggs Plant, 1940's

A New Project

Tom also moved on with his life. During the estrangement, he had decided that to keep himself agreeably occupied, he would build a mountain retreat in New Hampshire that would be his summer home. His plans were grand. This retreat would incorporate a model farm, homes for employees, gate houses, stables, and a comfortable home for Tom overlooking the lakes and mountains. Tom's brother William had a summer home in nearby Tuftonboro. He and his family encouraged Tom to buy Ossipee Mountain Park, a beautiful property a few miles away in Moultonborough that featured scenic views and trails. Ossipee Mountain Park was the former home of Benjamin F. Shaw who, in 1879 began developing over 360 acres of land surrounding the famous Ossipee Falls as his summer home. Shaw's home, "Weelahka Hall," had become a popular vacation resort and was visited by poets John Greenleaf Whittier and Lucy Larcom. Mr. Shaw had improved the mountain road and built paths and trails up the mountain and along Shannon Brook to a series of scenic water falls. He then opened Ossipee Park to the public and charged a small entrance fee.

After Shaw's death his family continued hosting guests until the property was sold to Emma F. Pettingill and Anna M. Olsson of New York who operated Weelahka Hall as a boarding house until 1911 when they placed the property for sale.

Early in the spring of 1911 Tom decided to act on his brother's recommendation. His secretary, Alfred H. Handley, William O. Robinson, James E. French and his brother William were a few of the agents who initially acquired this and other properties for him so he could hide his identity from the local land owners. Caroline, of course, was aware of the purchases of land in Moultonborough as she was listed on some of the deeds as his wife. Tom's extensive purchases of land and farms continued for many years until he had amassed over 6,600 acres.[182]

Leander Pynn, who became Tom Plant's general supervisor for the new summer estate and also his chauffeur, related his involvement in the secrecy for some of these meetings. When Mr. Plant came to Meredith from New York by train, he would call ahead for Pynn to meet the train with the small Cadillac he kept in Pynn's Meredith garage. "I would meet him at the station and drive him to Moultonborough where he would meet Jim French, (George) Blanchard and Will Robinson. They would talk awhile and then we would start out. All the Cadillac had were acetylene lights and I had to turn them out so the neighbors would not see us and begin to wonder what was going on. Mr. Plant made all the arrangements to take over a large amount of land before anything broke to let people know who was buying the land."[183]

Tom selected the Crow's Nest, a small observation pavilion at the top of the hill, as the site for his house which would be called Lucknow. The views of the lakes and the mountains were spectacular from this vantage point.

The Crow's Nest

Falls of Song

Mary's Arch

Bridal Veil Falls

The land around the Shaw property on the mountain had been a 19th century farming settlement called Ossipee Glen and included the Lee, Roberts, Whitten, Witham, (H)Orne, and Copp families and at its peak were forty strong. There were small family graves sprinkled around the homesites and at one time a school was built to educate the children. For many, the chance to sell their property was a welcome opportunity, but for the Lee family, the proposal to sell out and leave the farm on the mountain where five generations had lived was unwelcome. They fought to keep their homestead.

The prospect of country living in the Ossipee Mountains of New Hampshire made Tom Plant eager to begin the design of his home. To understand Plant's feelings about the land he had purchased, one has only to read his words as presented several years later by E. D. L. Seymour in the February 1917 Issue of *The New Country Life* —

"It isn't merely the mountains themselves," he explained, "though they give me every opportunity for outdoor life, for riding and driving and hunting, for buoyant health and a permanent constructive interest in things; it is more what they enable me to see and to experience as I contemplate from below their rugged bulk or stand on their lonely heights and try to take in the splendor of the outlook that stretches away around me. The whole broad sweep of country and the unbroken dome of sky that dips to meet it, all become part of me, of my very being, and I a part of them. Mt. Washington, cloud turbaned, forty miles to the north, Moosilauke and Sunapee and faint Monadnock close upon four score miles away, the Presidential Range, the Belknap crests, the wide stretch of rolling, lake-dotted country that extends to the distant New England coast, and most of all the myriad beauties of Winnipesaukee itself, that from this elevation assume new dimensions, new charms, new personalities—all these are mine as I gaze upon them. And more, too, that cannot be expressed, but only felt and made part of one's life."

"I don't claim that it is architecturally consistent," said Mr. Plant, "it combines features that I have seen and like in the houses of Norway, of England, and of Switzerland. That heavy oak ridge pole is adapted from the Japanese, but it gives just the result and effect that I wanted. I worked out plans that would give me the kind of house I desired and one that belonged right here, and not a line had to be changed in the building, not a detail failed to satisfy us."[184]

In 1911, Tom traveled abroad with his niece Amy. They returned from England on Cunard's *Mauretania* arriving in New York City on July 28.[185] He made a similar trip the following year, gathering design ideas for his new home. But, this trip brought him more than ideas!

Olive Cornelia Dewey

In his second trip to Europe in as many years, Tom met a young woman who was traveling in Europe with relatives. Tom was obviously searching for a companion, and this pleasant and reserved young lady from Toulon, Illinois intrigued him. Olive Cornelia Dewey was 29 years old and although Tom misrepresented his age as 49 making him 20 years older than Olive rather than the actual 24 years, the age difference didn't seem to matter. Although they returned to New York from Europe on separate ships days apart in early September 1912, they clearly planned on seeing one another. Tom's courtship of Olive gave the planning of his new estate in Moultonborough added urgency. Although he was living in New York City, he was making frequent trips to New Hampshire to oversee the work to repair and build estate roads and prepare the site for his home on the mountain. It became important to quickly enlarge and renovate McDonald cottage along the Mountain Road frontage of his mountain property as a home base. This house was very conveniently located between the two mountain roads that accessed the Crow's Nest building site.

Olive Dewey returned to her home in Toulon, Illinois. Not a whisper of news about a courtship was mentioned in the local newspaper, "*The Stark County News*." It could be expected that the news of an impending marriage of a member of one of Toulon's leading families to a very wealthy celebrity whose divorce scandal was publicized from coast to coast should be kept under wraps. There was, however, a note in the "Short Locals" column in the newspaper that Mrs. Charles P. Dewey and daughter, Olive, were spending a few days in Chicago in early December. Perhaps they were preparing a trousseau.[186]

It might be assumed that Tom Plant arrived in Toulon to visit the Dewey family over the holidays. However, the news blackout existed not only in Toulon, but in Boston and New York, as well, for at least several months until the fall of 1913.

Toulon is the county seat of Stark County, Illinois in the northwest quadrant of the state. Peoria, 40 miles away, is the nearest large town. Several Dewey cousins from New Hampshire settled there in the mid-19th century. Olive's grandfather, Samuel Mills Dewey, was born in Hanover, New Hampshire in 1821. Her great-grandfather, Capt. Andrew Dewey, in addition to being a farmer, was a carpenter. He moved from his Hanover home to Enfield, New Hampshire, a few miles east of Hanover, where he had purchased a farm and established a saw and shingle mill. Later he, too, moved to Toulon where his construction skills were very useful in a growing community. Several Dewey families had lived within several miles of Dartmouth College along the Connecticut River in New Hampshire.[187] Many of the New Hampshire cousins traveled west to Illinois for the new opportunities for farming and commerce.

At the end of the Civil War, Samuel Dewey, a Toulon merchant, began loaning his customers money and in December 1865, the banking house of Dewey & Burge was formed by his son, Charles P. Dewey, and his sister's son, Samuel Burge. In time, another partner was added to the bank, William E. Gould, and the firm became Dewey, Burge & Gould.

In 1920, Olive's father would purchase the interests of his partners and the firm was renamed Charles P. Dewey & Sons. "Prominent among the enterprising, progressive and farsighted business men of Toulon is Charles P. Dewey, financier and banker, who for more than forty years has been identified with the moneyed interests of the county. He is honored and respected by all, not alone by reason of the success he has achieved but also owing to the straightforward business policy he has ever followed. Stark County numbers him among her native sons."[188]

Olive's mother, Flora Dunham Dewey, was the daughter of Esquire Daniel Dunham and Olive Hathaway Dunham, both very prominent citizens of Wayne, Illinois who had emigrated from New York state. Daniel Dunham imported Percheron draft horses from France and began a breeding and importing business in 1872, becoming the first president of the Percheron Society of America. Ten years later he had 40 brood mares and 80 head in all.[189] At the time of his death at age 90, *The Chicago Live Stock World* in their November 28, 1910 issue had this to say about him. "His love for the soil was proved by his continuous residence of sixty years on his farm…A more picturesque personality never graced an industry. He was an industrious planter of forest and orchard trees, and at one time chartered a sailing vessel and brought down an entire cargo of growing evergreen trees from Mackinac Island, Michigan with which northern Illinois roadways and farms were beautified."[190]

The Dewey's had six children. Olive was firstborn, followed by her sister, Irene about two years later. Sadly, Irene died when Olive was six. The family expanded with brothers Mills Dunham, Charles Philip and Maurice Adams and a second sister, Marilla who was fifteen years younger than Olive.

Olive's Mother Flora with Marilla and Maurice

Olive and her siblings attended a local private college preparatory high school, the Toulon Academy, where Olive was the class valedictorian. She left home in the fall of 1901 to major in Greek at Wellesley College in Massachusetts.[191]

Returning home following her graduation from Wellesley with skills in not only Greek, but Latin and German, Olive began to teach at Toulon Academy. She stayed on the faculty until the Academy closed its doors in 1912. Then, she made a trip to Europe that changed her life.

She had fallen in love with a retired industrialist twenty-four years her senior.

Marilla and Olive Dewey

Both Tom and Olive returned to New York from Europe days apart early in September 1912. Catharine Haberley had arrived from England a few days earlier on August 31, 1912.

When Tom began purchasing the New Hampshire properties, he was estranged from Caroline. Now, in the fall of 1912, he had the pleasant prospect of sharing this beautiful spot with Olive Dewey with whom he was soon to begin a new life.

DESIGNING LUCKNOW

Tom's travels filled him with numerous design ideas. He realized that the "crow's nest" hilltop was relatively small and the siting of the house would be challenging. To incorporate his ideas into a coherent design that would provide the comfort and satisfaction that he desired, Tom needed a very special architect. The Boston architectural firm Shepley, Rutan and Coolidge, a successor to the Henry Hobson Richardson firm, began work on plans for the estate Tom Plant had envisioned.[192] But, there was a conflict of ideas and Tom looked for another architect who might work more compatibly with his suggestions.

Fortunately, he found J. Williams Beal, a very well known Boston architect. Beal had worked his way through MIT and was a member of the first class of its architectural school to study steel erection. The *MIT Tech Review* had this to say about his personality, "He impressed his professors and his fellow classmates with his ability of his work in the various problems presented, and his genial personality and good nature always made the tasks seem much easier."[193] After graduating from MIT, Beal worked in New York City as a draughtsman for Richard Morris Hunt, hired because of his knowledge of the use of steel in construction, and later for McKim, Mead and White.[194] Both of these firms were designing very distinguished mansions and town houses for prestigious clients in New York City, Newport and elsewhere. Following his work in New York, Beal made an extended European tour studying architecture.[195] He worked in a variety of styles including Classical, Colonial, Romanesque, Gothic, and Queen Anne. His flexibility and openness to Plant's suggestions made him a perfect architect for this project.

J. Williams Beal began his investigation of the site Tom had selected for his home. Beal understood the pull of the mountains and the wish to live near them and to enjoy the changing landscape. Several years earlier in 1908, Beal had designed a small rustic bungalow for Charles A. Burdett in Intervale, New Hampshire. He had incorporated a roofline in that small home that evoked a Japanese flavor.[196] Late in November 1912, Beal spent a week in New York City with Tom. His wife Mollie's (Mary) diary noted on November 28 "Papa home this A.M. 7:43 train - great time with Mr. Plant - Good Thanksgiving."[197]

Records kept and shared by Beal's family have given us the history of meetings between Plant and Beal as they designed an eclectic Arts and Crafts bungalow of 16 rooms on Plant's most perfect site. The entire project was going to be a Gentleman's Country Estate and Model Farm and a very typical example of the Country House Movement of the era. The farm was to be self sustaining and self sufficient.

J. Williams Beal was born May 19, 1855 in South Scituate, Massachusetts and died July 07, 1919 in Hanover, Massachusetts. He graduated from the MIT School of Architecture in 1877.

Beal Family History

Tom Plant had construction experience with the expansion of his manufacturing plants and had ideas and the background to make suggestions for his home. There was no question that Tom planned on being involved. The design of the building demonstrated Beal's engineering skills as he employed a structural system of steel beams and concrete slab floors along with hollow structural terra cotta blocks that formed the exterior and some interior walls. The terra cotta block construction, while expensive, was considered fireproof and also provided insulation for the building.[198] The exterior blocks were hidden behind a veneer of native Conway (pink) granite. Hand-hewn oak beams, heavy rafter tails and half timbering completed the appearance of an eclectic English Arts and Crafts bungalow that Beal had designed for Plant.[199]

Early in the planning stages, discussions ensued about the addition of an Aeolian organ. A residential organ was a symbol of status and was almost a necessity for the well-appointed millionaire's home. Aeolian Opus 1257 was ordered on March 31, 1913, and the space for its installation was part of the floor plans.[200] Additionally, Tom ordered an Aeolienne, an organ roll player. He planned on using this mechanism to play the organ himself.

Beal was only four years older than Tom, but had suffered a stroke in 1912. His son, John Woodbridge Beal, became his assistant and accompanied him on his visits to the building site in New Hampshire. On several occasions while the plans were being developed, John Woodbridge Beal joined Tom in his private railcar in the Providence railroad station when Tom's train the "Empire Limited" stopped on its northbound trip from New York to Boston. A porter carried the bundles of drawings for them to work on while Tom's car was being switched from Boston's South Station to North Station and the connection to Meredith, New Hampshire.[201]

Although dyslexic, John had earned a degree/certificate from MIT for his experience in the field along with courses at Northeastern University that he took while working with his father and met the requirements for AIA membership. His father's helpful advice was to focus on the functionality of a building. John was a "whiz at math" and managed the business side of his father's projects.[202] He also got along very well with businessmen and produced work on budget and on time.[203] His brother, Horatio (Ray) W. Beal, graduated from Harvard with a master's degree in architecture in 1915 and joined his father and brother in the firm. Beginning in July 1913 Ray accompanied his father to the Plant project in NH and through 1914 as well.[204] Their brother, Bob, was a landscape architect and consulted on the project, too. He had studied and worked with Frederick Law Olmsted, Jr.[205] Several of his garden designs have become landmarks. Following their father's death in 1919, the brothers formed the architectural firm, J. Williams Beal, Sons in 1920.

By the middle of March 1911, Tom's new neighbors in Moultonborough knew who he was, the Jamaica Plain millionaire shoe manufacturer. Many of the local people weren't thrilled by all the activity on the mountain, their mountain. Thomas Kelly, of the John Kelly Contracting Company, who was in charge of the site preparation, brought five car loads of dump carts and thirty-five draught horses and three hundred laborers to Moultonborough to begin the work that Tom Plant had laid out.[206] It was known by March that Tom had purchased three thousand acres and work on the property had begun immediately. Fred E. Ellis, a well-known road builder from Melrose, Massachusetts, was beginning extensive roadwork. And, Ossipee Park was closed due to the construction.[207]

The Italian laborers hired to work on the building site and roads caused a great panic in August when sixty of them rioted after they were paid off, but not given the fare to return to Boston. They'd been concerned when the work slowed down, and they were doing odd jobs rather than the work they'd been employed to do. They were fearful the job wasn't going to last. Armed with pistols and knives, they rioted and threatened the safety of the townspeople and summer residents. Those residents who had carriages and automobiles fled in terror. Governor Bass was called on to send out the militia. Instead he called Herbert Burke, the high sheriff of Carroll County in nearby Madison, who borrowed a car and quickly gathered a posse of his deputies armed with hunting rifles to calm the men and escort them to a boat at Melvin Point. They were taken across the lake to the Weirs train station and sent by rail to Boston.[208]

Note: On August 4, 1919 a suit was filed in the Suffolk County Superior Court by the John Kelly Contracting Company for $75,000 against Thomas G. Plant alleging breach of contract.[209] This suit was finally settled in February 1922 with a verdict for the plaintiff for $2,370.33 for work done.[210]

COMMUNITY FEELINGS

Meanwhile, Martha Lee would not sell her farm. In December, men working for Tom Plant, presumably with his knowledge, crudely painted parts of the still standing Weelahka Hall and summer house with black paint and built a 20' high haphazard fence running several hundred feet across from her property to block her view of the mountains. This "spite fence" painted with grotesque figures and drawings of currency was designed to shame her into selling her family farm so that Tom could complete his land holdings on the mountain.[211] William Henry Horne, who had lived with the Lees for more than 35 years, in an interview in the *Boston Globe* the following February, said that he, too, had a lot on the mountain, but Tom hadn't offered enough money for him to sell out either. He noted Martha Lee had turned down $3,000 from her relatives for her house and land the past summer so Plant's offer of $2,500 certainly wasn't acceptable.[212] The hostility escalated when men working for Plant began to remove gravestones from the Lee Family Cemetery. The Moultonborough selectmen quickly stepped in to stop this illegal desecration of the graveyard. For some, Tom Plant would always be remembered as a bully.

Curiosity consumed the local community. What kind of man was this, what did he want? George Bacon, a local Wolfeboro writer, summoned the courage to meet with Tom Plant to try to find out. The following is a part of the story Bacon published in the local *Granite State News* on January 13, 1912.

"Mr. Plant is a very pleasant gentleman to meet. He did not know he was being interviewed, but supposed he was talking to a representative of one of the farm owners in the region he is seeking to develop, so it is but fair to assume that he talked business, instead of talking for mere publication.

" 'Drive people from their farms? Not a bit of it!' said Mr. Plant. 'Quite the contrary. It is no desire of mine to gain possession of a big tract of country made up by the consolidation of many adjoining farms from which the former owners have been expelled. I would very much prefer that every desirable family remain in occupancy after they have sold out to me. What do I mean by desirable family? I mean just what you or any other decent person would mean. I mean a typical New England family, industrious and self-respecting. I have no use for loafers, for drunkards or for worthless people of any kind, but I have a great deal of use for the man or for the family that believes in a square deal for all and will act accordingly.'

" 'No, I make no pretension that my motive in seeking to develop this region is at all philanthropic. I hope and believe that the successful carrying out of my plans will be of great benefit to the people. I hope and believe that the benefit will not be confined to this immediate vicinity, but still I make no claim that my main reason for carrying out the project is to serve the public.'

" 'No, I am not acting for a syndicate, in spite of rumors to the contrary. The simple truth is that I am going into this for the fun of the thing. That is, I want to keep Thomas G. Plant agreeably occupied. He has always been a busy person. For a good many years he had to literally hustle for a living. Now that he has retired from active business, he must still keep busy at something - for habit is second nature - and as he knows that for him the mere pursuit of pleasure would be as hopeless and fruitless as a wild goose chase, he intends to seek some diversion in the development of the possibilities of this region as a place of beauty and also as a stock-raising and farming section.'

" 'For I love outdoor life. I am a great admirer of nature, and I shall find much pleasure in making easily accessible various points from which to observe the remarkable natural beauty of this region to the best possible advantage. That means, among other things, the building of roads to peaks on Ossipee mountain - roads so graded as to make the use of them a pleasure instead of a toilsome task, roads so arranged as to make the transit from lake to mountain an easy matter.'

" 'In the matter of stock-raising there is opportunity for much pleasurable occupation and worth-while accomplishment. This is not a rich farming country, never has been and never can be, but it affords opportunity for successful stock-raising and also for the growing of apples and for other varieties of fruit culture, and it is my hope and expectation to be given the chance to demonstrate beyond the possibility of reasonable doubt that the result of intelligent work in this section of New England will richly reward the up-to-date stock raiser or fruit grower.'

" 'But do not misunderstand me. This is not a get-rich-quick scheme of mine. I know that, even if my plans are not interfered with by inability to purchase desired lands at prices I feel I can afford to pay, a number of years will have passed before the income from the sale of livestock, fruits and other products will equal the expense of maintenance. But my return for the expenditure of time, thought and money I devote to the project will come in the shape of agreeable occupation, of feeling that I am bringing about genuine and permanent improvement in prevailing conditions, of attracting and retaining desirable resident families. Every man with real red blood in his veins likes to feel that he is of some actual use in the world. It would be a source of abiding satisfaction to me to know that one result of my work in this region was the affording of actual proof of the wisdom of the slogan, "back to the farm," when rightfully interpreted.' "[213]

An Involved Life

Tom had been living in New York City off and on since 1909, traveling back and forth to Boston and later in 1911 to New Hampshire to check on his business interests, investments, and the construction of his mountain retreat. He was comfortably settled in the Hotel Gotham at the corner of Fifth Avenue and 55th Street. The hotel was arranged similarly to the Somerset with guest rooms and suites of apartments. Built in 1905, the Gotham was originally designed as an elegant home for wealthy patrons. When he was in France in 1912, he purchased and shipped to New York a Model 30 Packard limousine for his use in the city.[214] His chauffeur, Leander Pynn, describes the car, "it had one of those half windshields so that the chauffeur was exposed to all the weather. I had to have a rubber hat and coat as well as winter clothing when I drove to New York".[215]

1912 Packard Limousine, Model 30

Legal Involvements

In 1911, Tom was involved in court cases. Although not directly involved in the Federal Government's trial in the spring of 1912 to dissolve the United Shoe Machinery Company, he would have been following it with a great deal of interest. He was the defendant in Harry W. Smith's suit for a 5% commission for bringing about the sale of Plant's shoe and machinery business to United Shoe. The jury in this case awarded Smith $323,750 for his commission and interest. Plant planned to appeal.[216] On January 17, 1911, James A. Hutchinson, a note broker, brought a $150,000 suit against Plant for his services in securing a loan of $3,000,000 from several investors. The jury returned a verdict of $109,168.[217]

Political Involvement

Tom was active politically, too. He raised $20,000 for Theodore Roosevelt's 1912 Presidential race against William Howard Taft. Tom knew Theodore Roosevelt as he'd been asked by the National Shoemakers Association to intercede with the President to reduce the leather tariff during Roosevelt's first term in office. The two men had similar interests. Both enjoyed hunting in New Brunswick, fishing in northern Maine and riding fast horses anywhere. It can only be speculated that they might have met while pursuing these sporting activities. What did intrigue Tom was Theodore Roosevelt's success in breaking up trusts, beginning in 1904 with J. P. Morgan's Northern Securities Company, a railroad trust. Roosevelt had gained fame as a "trustbuster" although he was really interested in regulating business behavior. In the years following this first case, his administration brought forward a number of antitrust cases. Theodore Roosevelt's hand-picked successor, William Howard Taft, had disappointed Roosevelt and many of his Republican friends. They convinced the former President to run against Taft on the Progressive ticket, splitting the Republican vote and thus ensuring the Democrat, Woodrow Wilson, would become the next President.

Investments

While there's no doubt he had been a successful investor, many of his investments were not known or were a matter of speculation. He had three million dollars of United Shoe Machinery Company stock and another three million dollars in cash from the sale of his shoe business interests. It has been reported that he was also involved in the futures markets. J. Williams Beal's grandson learned from his father that Tom was investing in leather futures.[218] His opinion on leather prices and the German market for hides was quoted in an article in the *New York Times* and on market price in the *Wall Street Journal*.[219] In fact, his business opinion was often sought and published. Another of the speculative investments that became part of the historical lore was sugar. A number of sugar companies were headquartered in Boston and information about them would have been available to Tom through his business and banking partnerships. Sugar futures rose and fell spectacularly in what became known as the "Dance of the Millions." During World War I the sugar beet crops in Europe were decimated by the fighting in the beet fields, and the market began to rely on cane sugar. Cuba became the biggest sugar producer in the world. Olive and Tom travelled to Cuba in 1917 and were again in Palm Beach that same year.[220] In November, 1920 the demand for Cuban sugar swiftly decreased as Europe's beet sugar fields and factories recovered from WWI's (1914-1918) devastation.[221] Not only did Cuban banks fail, American speculators who had rushed to Cuba to buy land, lost their investment. Tom Plant was among them.

It has been said that President Roosevelt recommended to Tom the purchase of Imperial Russian Bonds. Certainly the President would have known that the Czarist government needed investment very badly after the Russo-Japanese War was settled in 1905. Roosevelt was directly involved in negotiating the Peace Treaty which ended this war and was awarded the Nobel Peace Prize for his effort. Tom purchased Imperial bonds with a face value of $700,000. The Bolshevik revolution in 1917 made these bonds practically worthless. However, the bond certificates remained in his possession and became part of his estate. As administratrix of the estate, Olive received $4,372 for the bonds in 1941.[222]

1913 — 1914

With a business life in New York City, a massive building project in New Hampshire, a couple of legal appeals, and an upcoming marriage, Tom's life was busy and exciting. He had always managed to balance a full schedule and this was no different. Early in February, the U.S. Supreme Court unanimously held that United Machinery was not in violation of the Sherman anti-trust law by nature of its organization, but the structure of the leases and the "tying clause" were not before the court for consideration.[223] This disappointment was followed by the Harry Smith lawsuit decision which had had him in court in Worcester, Massachusetts in March. The Massachusetts Supreme Court sustained the verdict for Smith in October 1913.[224] The James Hutchinson lawsuit followed on April 22 in Salem, Massachusetts. The earlier verdict was also sustained. And, on Tuesday, April 29, Caroline Plant was given a Decree Absolute in Boston, ending Tom and Caroline's marriage.

Now that they were free to marry, Tom and Olive moved quickly. Four days later on the following Saturday, May 3, 1913, Edward J. S. Brown from Midvale, New Jersey and Helen B. Kalbfus, from Shohola, Pennsylvania were the witnesses to their marriage performed in the parsonage by Thomas J. Clark, pastor of the United Methodist Church in Midvale, Prompton Township, New Jersey[225] [226] They were busy

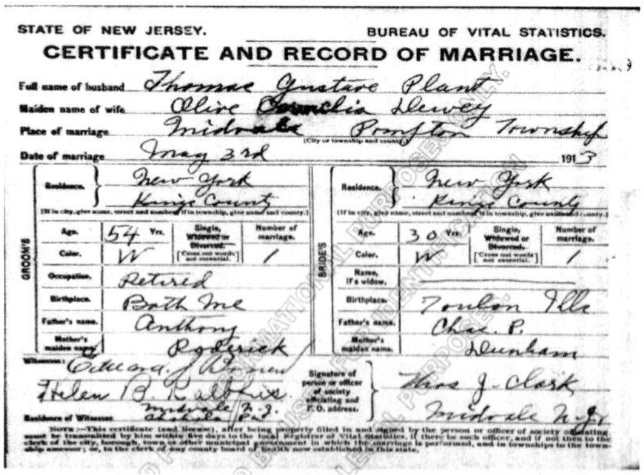
STATE OF NEW JERSEY. BUREAU OF VITAL STATISTICS.

CERTIFICATE AND RECORD OF MARRIAGE.

Full name of husband: Thomas Gustave Plant
Maiden name of wife: Olive Cornelia Dewey
Place of marriage: Midvale Prompton Township (City or township and county)
Date of marriage: May 3rd 1913

GROOM'S		BRIDE'S	
Residence	New York, Kings County	Residence	New York, Kings County
Age	54 Yrs.	Age	30 Yrs.
Color	W	Color	W
Single, Widowed or Divorced		Single, Widowed or Divorced	
Number of marriage	1	Number of marriage	1
Occupation	Retired	Name, if a widow	
Birthplace	Bath Me	Birthplace	Toulon Ills
Father's name	Anthony	Father's name	Chas. P.
Mother's maiden name	Roderick	Mother's maiden name	Dunham

Witnesses: Edward J. Brown, Helen B. Kalbfus
Residence of Witnesses: Midvale N.J., Shohola Pa.
Signature of person or officer of society officiating and P.O. address: Thos J. Clark, Midvale N.J.

NOTE.—This certificate (and license), after being properly filled in and signed by the person or officer of society officiating must be transmitted by him within five days to the local Registrar of Vital Statistics, if there be such officer, and if not then to the clerk of the city, borough, town or other municipal government in which the marriage is performed, and in townships to the township assessor; or, to the clerk of any county board of health now established in this state.

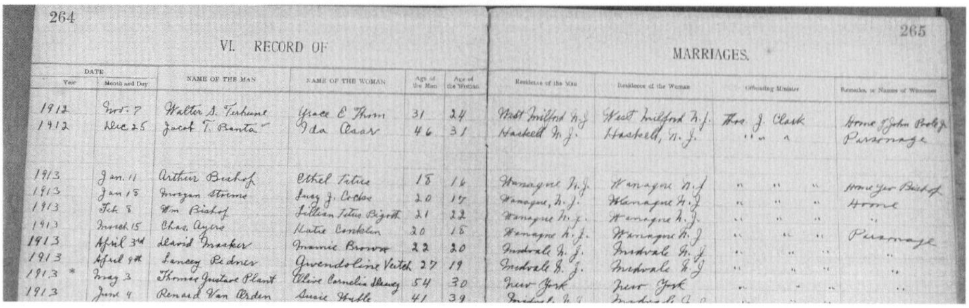
264 VI. RECORD OF MARRIAGES. 265

Date: Year	Month and Day	Name of the Man	Name of the Woman	Age of the Man	Age of the Woman	Residence of the Man	Residence of the Woman	Officiating Minister	Remarks, or Names of Witnesses
1912	Nov. 7	Walter S. Terhune	Grace E Thom	31	24	West Milford N.J.	West Milford N.J.	Thos J. Clark	Home of John Poole
1912	Dec 25	Jacob T. Banta	Ida Osar	46	31	Haskell N.J.	Haskell, N.J.	" "	Parsonage
1913	Jan. 11	Arthur Bishof	Ethel Titus	18	16	Wanaque N.J.	Wanaque N.J.	" " "	Home Geo Bishof
1913	Jan 18	Morgan Storms	Inez J. Cocker	20	17	Wanaque, N.J.	Wanaque N.J.	" " "	Home
1913	Feb. 8	Wm Bishof	Lillian Titus Bigott	21	22	Wanaque N.J.	Wanaque N.J.	" " "	"
1913	March 15	Chas. Ayers	Katie Conklin	20	18	Wanaque N.J.	Wanaque N.J.	" " "	
1913	April 3rd	David Masker	Mamie Brown	22	20	Midvale N.J.	Midvale N.J.	" " "	Parsonage
1913	April 9th	Lancey Redner	Gwendoline Veitch	27	19	Midvale N.J.	Midvale N.J.	" " "	"
1913 *	May 3	Thomas Gustave Plant	Olive Cornelia Dewey	54	30	New York	New York	" " "	"
1913	June 4	Renard Van Orden	Susie Hubble	41	39	Midvale N.J.	Midvale N.J.	" " "	"

selecting and buying furnishings for the new house when they were in New York. However, the summer and fall months made the clean fresh air and beauty of New Hampshire a joyful retreat. The remodeled McDonald cottage was the perfect spot for them to live during the estate construction. After a European honeymoon in the spring, Tom and Olive returned to find part of the new estate road had been made wider than the single lane Tom had specified. This two mile roadway, built by Fred E. Ellis, an MIT-educated mechanical engineer and master road builder from Massachusetts, was carefully constructed through the woods, paralleling Shannon Brook until it began the gradual ascent with switchbacks for steeper areas to maintain a gentle grade. The estate road ended on the level plateau at the Carriage House. The road from the Carriage House to the site for the main house on the Crow's Nest was carved out of the side of the rocky hill and wound around it as it ascended. Ellis crowned the new road beds for drainage, added culverts to manage storm water and carefully built up the road with crushed rock and compacted layers of stone dust to provide a hard macadam surface suitable for all wheeled vehicles. He continued building roads throughout the estate up to the tops of the mountains. On the mountain roads, all necessary drainage was built of hand-laid stone tunnels with small rock to slow down erosion where permanent streams existed.[227] Ellis did remake the Estate road as a single lane as Tom had wished.

The model farm was one of his first construction projects. Tom was anxious to get the farm complex up and running to provide shelter and food for the village of workers on the estate. The large German-Swiss style barn was completed in 1913. The seven-room cottage built for farm workers would have been one of the many buildings used to temporarily house the men and women working on the estate who were housed in all the available buildings including Weelahka Hall and its annex.

The Construction Community

Having 600 to 1000 workers living and working on the estate must have had an impact on the life of this small rural community. When you think of the small village they were constructing, the numbers made sense. Olive Plant added her memories about the early days in correspondence with Elizabeth Crawford Wilkin for her 1964 book *The Castle And The Club, The Bald Peak Colony Club.* "The plans were worked over during the winter of 1912 and 1913, and in the spring the work was started. Tom was impatient to have it completed and so employed nearly 1000 men, mostly Italian mason workers, but some carpenters, of course, and about 50 teamsters. The teamsters lived in Weelahka Hall… most of them came from the surrounding country but some from Boston. The Italian masons all came from Boston. They were expert stone masons and so built the house, stables, the two lodges and miles of stone walls, particularly where the property ran along the highway. They also worked on the 30 miles of road which were laid out by Mr. Plant and an engineer. This entailed great exertion as there was no way of getting over the mountain except by walking, often re-tracing their steps to find the best way to circumvent a steep climb.

"The Italians also worked on the 9-hole golf course, and on a stone dam to impound the waters from the stream which was the source of Shannon Brook. This made a small lake and gave fine fishing. The stream itself was a natural trout stream."

An article in the Laconia *News and Critic* on July 23 describes activity at the construction site, "two steam trucks belonging to the company, ply back and forth between Meredith and Ossipee, transporting freight of all descriptions. L. G. Flynn [Pynn] & Co. have a Pierce Arrow '08 touring car remodeled into a huge truck which hauls principally beer and bread, to be consumed by the hundreds of Italians that swarm over the mountain…the food served at the hotel consists mainly of stews and roasts, the same cuts being used for both. Seldom does any steak find its way to the tables, yet the food is clean and wholesome and contains nourishment enough for rugged, energetic men. The community at the present time is composed of six hundred men and four girls. No one is allowed on the mountain who does not work in some capacity for Mr. Plant, or have business there. It has been reported that already 15 miles of state road have been completed on the estate and the foundation for the $500,000 house is nearly finished."

New Boathouse

Weelahka Hall

Maple Lodge - Upper Gatehouse

Lucknow Under Construction

Note: The photos of the building site and the life of some of the workers engaged there were gathered by Arthur Landry who was a finish flooring carpenter who worked for the R. T. Adams Co. Hardwood Floors, Springfield and Boston. The photos were loaned by Arthur Landry's grandson. Bruce Reynolds, Meredith, New Hampshire.

Two of Olive's brothers, Maurice and Phil Dewey, came east from Illinois and got jobs as time keepers during two summers. Being part of this big construction job must have been exciting for these two.

Maurice Dewey, age 17

Six months after the fact, the newspapers discovered Tom's remarriage and all the headlines had a similar theme that Tom was building a "castle" for his bride. Beginning in 1913 Tom's home was referred to as the "castle" even in town records.

Over the Christmas holidays, Tom and Olive traveled to Toulon, Illinois and stayed with her parents. Tom returned to New York and left Olive in Illinois to have a longer visit with her parents and family.[228]

Materials of Construction

Between one hundred and one hundred and thirty million years ago, the Ossipee Mountains had a very different look. What appear to be individual peaks today are actually what is left of a large, now extinct volcano. A second eruption created the famous ring dike. The outer ring is an almost perfect circle of granite nine miles in diameter.[229] Thomas Plant built his home, Lucknow, on the lower western slopes below Mt. Shaw and Mt. Roberts.

The columnar basalt formation on nearby Bald Mountain and Turtle Back Mountain that resulted from the volcano may have informed Tom Plant's decision to have the veneer facing his home cut into 5 and 6 sided shapes reminiscent of columnar structure.

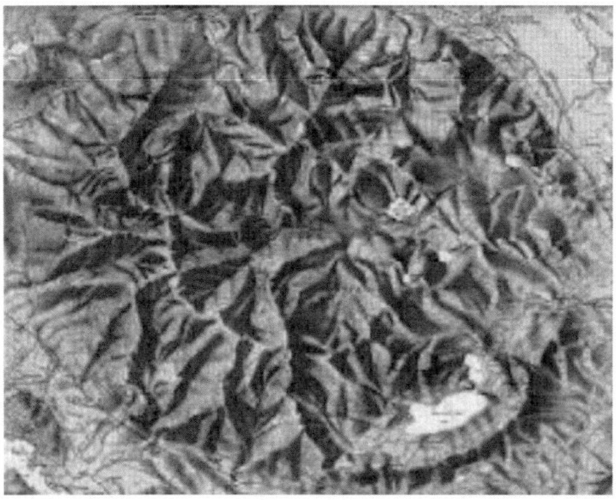

Ring Dike

Columnar Structure

The rocks that Tom used for the buildings were a combination of rhyolite and the pinkish Conway granite found on the site and locally in both Carroll and Belknap Counties. In building Lucknow the stone masons shaped each stone to lock together. They were mostly flush at the edges but crowned at the center of the face of each stone.[230]

The Redstone Quarry in Conway, New Hampshire was the likely source of the veneer stone used on the buildings.[231] The quarried, finely cut edged stone veneer, averaged four to six inches in depth.[232] A railroad spur in the quarry connected with the Maine Central Railroad. Quarried stone for Plant's property would have been taken by rail south

40 miles to Ossipee and then trucked to the construction site. Smaller pieces of the same stone continued on the Maine Central line to Bath, Maine and were delivered to the William T. Donnell Ship Yard. Here, workmen fashioned oak timbers for the half-timbered sections and cut the stone to fill the half-timbered gables and dormers with the same matching pink Conway granite used in the rest of the building.

Tom contacted Scott R. Frye, his close boyhood friend in Bath, to acquire $75,000 of white oak. Mr. Frye was the proprietor of the Bath Auto & Gas Engine Company and had a construction business on the side. After obtaining the contract, Frye turned the project over to his building superintendent, Fred Larrabee, a well-known Maine boat builder and contractor. Fred oversaw the fashioning of the oak timbers used in the half-timbered sections of the building. They were fastened with handmade treenails (wooden pegs) in the same manner used in the construction of wooden boats.[233]

The Donnell shipyard located on Washington Street in Bath, Maine was the site where 35 to 40, "veteran carpenters assembled the oak framework, along with the window frames, gables, etc. then took them apart and they were shipped to Ossipee Mountain. Mr. Larrabee recalls that one dormer roof window weighed five tons and one of the gables required an entire flatcar for shipment."[234] The shipyard had all the necessary overhead cranes to move these heavy materials once they were completed and to load them on railcars for transport to New Hampshire.

"Mr. Plant wanted the oak, wherever exposed, to resemble a pattern such as presented by hen feathers. Hence, it had to have an adze finish and for days the veteran shipwrights experienced with the razor sharp adze (worked) to hit on a design suitable to the client. Finally, Horatio Douglas turned forth the specimen accepted."[235] Among the men also working in the shipyard were the stone masons who chiseled and rusticated the stone to fill the half timbered sections. These masons were from an island near Sable Island and Halifax, Nova Scotia.[236]

The oak framework was shipped by rail to Alton, New Hampshire at the southern end of Lake Winnipesaukee and sent by barge to Plant's lakeside property in Moultonborough. From there, teams of oxen brought the finished materials up the mountain to the building site.

LUCKNOW

"Sited on a ledgy outcrop, it stands out as exemplary of the Arts and Crafts movement. It features horizontal lines and lies low to the ground with a low-pitched roof and broad overhanging eaves - all intended to ensure it blended in with the surrounding, rugged landscape. Exterior walls are faced with distinctively shaped stone quarried locally and clay tiles in muted hues cover the roof. Oversized wooden brackets with shaped and incised ends, mortise-and-tenoned oak timbers whose exposed surfaces were hand hewn with a curved chisel and Medieval-type half-timbering."[237]

Sited on a Ledgy Outcrop

The half timbered sections of wood were fashioned to resemble trees and the stone walls slightly flared at the base of the building resembling the roots of trees rising up from the soil. Both are nice Arts and Crafts details. The house seemed to nestle right into the site.

The Mountain Porch

Flared (Battered) Stone Walls

Windows and doors were English casements with thick leaded glass panes, some with painted roundels that reflected the exterior landscape or sporting activities enjoyed on the estate.

Josiah L. Lawrence was the superintendent of the construction firm "Bigelow & Harriman, contractors for building the large summer residence, lodges, stables, gardener's dwellings etc., for the multimillionaire, Mr. Thomas G. Plant."[238] This firm specialized in 'good residential work' but also industrial plant construction and had offices in both Boston and New York.

Tom suggested ideas from his days as a manufacturer. He added seven skylights on the roof. They brought natural light into the attic area and when panels of glass were added to the ceilings of darkened hallways on the second floor, the area brightened. One large frame of glass panels was installed in the upstairs stair hall. Here, Tiffany stained glass panes in blue and pale yellow filtered the natural daylight from the skylights and bathed the hall in a wonderful, warm inviting light.

Tiffany Stained Glass in the Upstairs Stair Hall

Lucknow Floor Plans

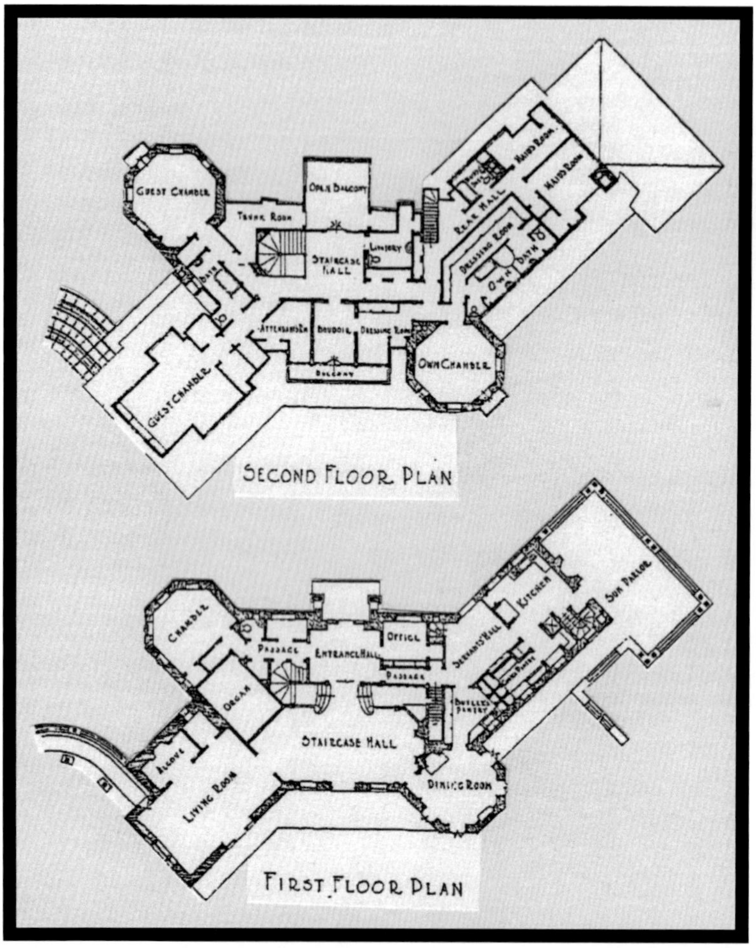

Every room had a wonderful view of the mountains or the lakes - Squam and Winnipesaukee. Fresh air came down from the mountainside and entered and cooled the house. Opposing French doors allowed the breezes to pass through the house. A sun porch anchored the southeast corner and served as a summer living room. It included a fireplace to add warmth on cool evenings.

Some ceilings were curved and the Dining Room ceiling was decorated with a domed plaster relief of wisteria flowers and vines - a striking design made of 57 pieces of cast plaster made from wood molds.

Both Tom and Olive had a love of flowers and gardening. Tom had installed a greenhouse at his shoe factory so that there would be fresh flowers for the desks of the workers. He had taken great pleasure in the "Noonday Rest Park" that had also been designed by Olmsted for the pleasure of his employees. Now, he planned a heated 100-foot Lord & Burnham greenhouse for his home.[239] It curved around the retaining wall on the south side of the house. Olive enjoyed working in it.

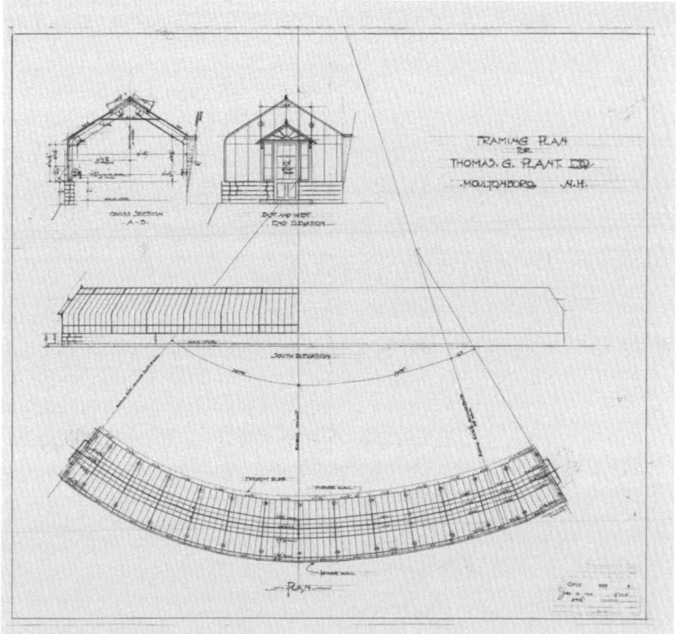

LUCKNOW

On a foot hill of the mountain
Stands a sturdy house of stone
On the lawn in front, a fountain;
And the house is vine o'ergrown..

For the eyes of those who dwell there
Nature has a wondrous feast;
A lovely lake lies in the distance,
Mountains to the West and East.

Guests who enter to this dwelling
Stand in wonder and amaze,
For such a view as is unfolded
Ne'er before has met their gaze.

To each guest there is presented
At this dwelling on the hill,
A varied list of pleasant pastimes,
Of which each may take his fill.

Does this one Angle? A ruffled lake
Presents its surface to his fly,
And each leaping trout that he pulls out
Spurs him on once more to try.

Does this one Golf? A rolling field
Covered with velvet of emerald sheen;
Constantly tempts him, lures him on
To try his skill at just one more green.

Does this one ride? A pleasant steed
Will carry him over the hills all day
Till evening comes with the setting sun,
Reminder, "Don't be too long away."

Does this one walk? A valley fair
Cradles a rushing impetuous stream,
And hearing its chatter and endless patter,
One wonders and watches its broken gleam.

So to each guest is his desire;
And when the day too soon has past,
In the twilit hall, by the open fire
Each one agrees, "I'm in Luck Now at last."

By Olive Dewey Plant

Plant Brothers & Company

With Lucknow's construction well underway, Tom Plant approached an associate, Alfred Grover, with a scheme that would benefit Grover and would place Tom's nephews in a position to be educated in the world of business. Tom had increasingly worried that William, Jr., young Tom, and Everett were quickly becoming playboys and needed guidance. Grover had been mentored by Tom as he built up his shoe manufacturing business in Lynn and had gained so much business acumen that Tom made him Purchasing Agent for the Thomas G. Plant Shoe Company when Grover was only twenty-three years old. Four years later he became a Director of the Company.

The proposal was that Tom Plant would be a silent partner in a women's shoe manufacturing business headquartered in Manchester, New Hampshire. Alfred Grover would be Vice President and General Manager and would teach Tom's nephews the business while he ran the company as his own. It helped that he had a good personal relationship with the boys. In fact, his young son, Paul Grover, had been a page in

Alfred Crosby Grover

At the time of his death at age 41, he was Vice President and General Manager of Plant Brothers & Company

their sister Amy's wedding. In addition, teaching came easily—he'd been giving lectures on the "Broad Science of Purchasing for Large

Corporations" at Boston University for several years. The deal between Tom and Alfred was that additional capital, if needed, would be supplied by Tom and at the end of five years, Alfred was to have the option to either take over the company in its entirety on his terms, or sell to the boys on equal terms.

By September 1916, as the United States was preparing to enter World War I, Grover saw the opportunity to use the sewing machines used in shoe manufacture to also manufacture military equipment. He won government contracts to supply cartridge belts, holsters, harnesses, feed and water bags for horses, haversacks, leggings, gas mask containers, and other army equipment. The company established factories in Manchester, NH, Boston, Lynn and Newburyport, MA, seven in all. They produced 11,000,000 pieces of military equipment made of leather and fabric during the war. The efficiency of their war effort earned a citation from the War Department. "A. C. Grover, general manager of the company, is in active charge, and his initiative and ability have been in good part responsible for the growth of the concern."[240]

Unfortunately, the strain of making weekly visits to all of the plants, interspersed with trips to Washington, DC wore Alfred down. On one of his trips to Washington he contracted typhoid fever. On August 24, 1920, just two weeks after returning from Washington, he died at the age of 41, leaving his wife and five young children.[241]

All three Plant brothers served in WW I, and William Franklin Plant, Jr., and Thomas Corey Plant on their return, became Treasurer and President of the Plant Brothers Company respectively. Everett Dunbar Plant, on his return, rejoined the Company in Manchester. After 1927, all evidence of the firm was gone and the brothers were no longer found in the Manchester City Directory.

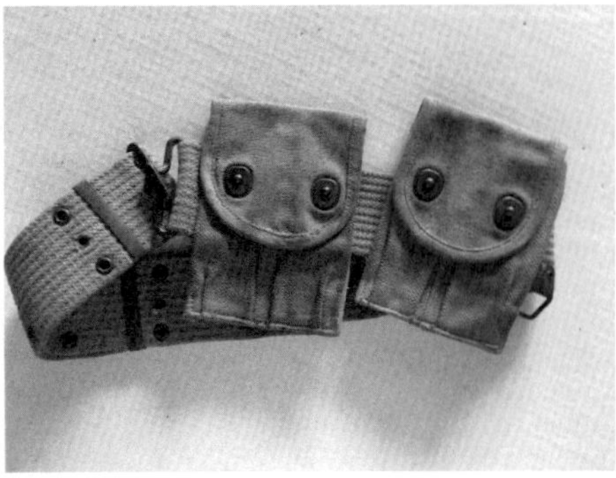

Plant Brothers & Company

Cartridge Belt and Clip Holders
PB & Co Aug. 1918 on belt
PB & Co Nov. 1918 on clip holder
PB & Co Jan. 1918 on 2nd clip holder

Busy 1914

Tom and Olive were in New York for the winter. There were a great many decisions to make about furnishing the house, and New York was a perfect city to find the companies with the most interesting furniture and objets d'art. Books, paintings, fabrics, rugs, carpets and furniture that exemplified a tradition of handicraft and artisanship were sought for their wonderful summer home. The Plant's chauffeur, Leander Pynn, wrote of the difficulties of finding parking places in New York while Mrs. Plant conducted her shopping forays. The Boston firm, Irving & Casson, was engaged to fit the interior of the first floor of Lucknow with elm paneling fastened with butterfly joints, carved beams, and built-in benches carved in a gothic style reminiscent of the work the firm had completed for churches. Irving & Casson's business card listed the complete services offered. Although a Boston firm, Irving and Casson had a 5th Avenue store in New York City. A majority of the furniture selected for the house was made by Irving & Casson — some pieces were designed for specific rooms.

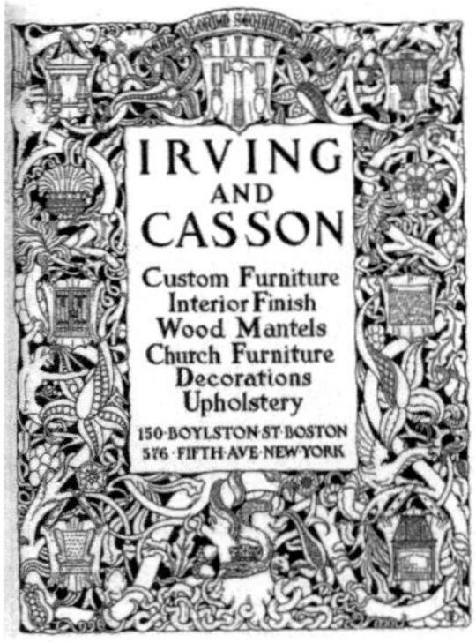

Irving and Casson Furniture - 1914

Perhaps the finest furniture ordered for Lucknow were those pieces that were labeled Tobey "Handmade" Furniture. They were handmade by skilled Norwegian craftsmen employed by the Tobey Furniture Company of Chicago and were sold only on one floor of the Chicago store and exclusively in a branch store on 5th Avenue at 53rd Street in New York City. The library table shown in the Tobey ad was ordered by the Plants with a berry and leaf pattern carved into the edge of the top rather than the plain edge shown in the ad. The Tobey Company didn't issue catalogues for the handmade line and showed its stock only in its stores. However, a beautifully printed booklet with a cover embossed in gilt lettering was sent to inquirers to induce those interested to visit either the Chicago or the New York store. Prices were not quoted as the time and labor could not be determined in advance. The company had the belief that most potential buyers of Tobey handmade furniture were able to visit either Chicago or New York, if contemplating purchasing something so costly.[242] The Plants ordered at least eleven pieces of Tobey Handmade Furniture.

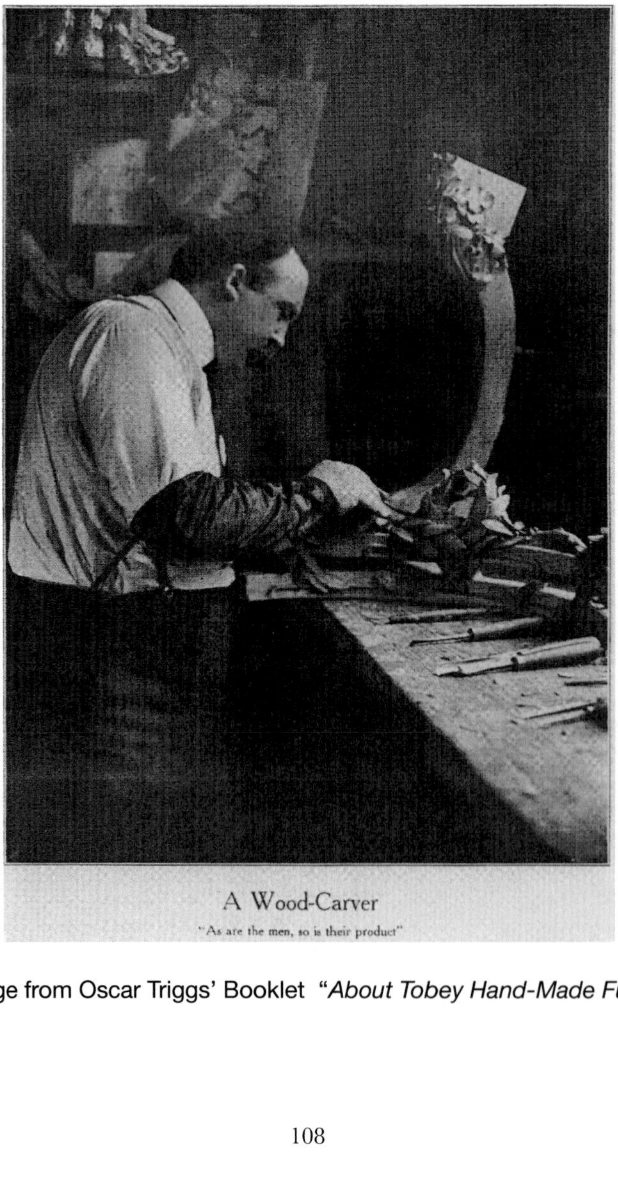

An Image from Oscar Triggs' Booklet *"About Tobey Hand-Made Furniture"*

Also featured were furnishings from the finest suppliers. Edward F. Caldwell & Co. in New York City supplied the light fixtures, P. E. Guerin, a New York company in business since 1857, cast all the bronze cabinet and door knobs for the house. The William H. Jackson Co., also in New York City, supplied the fireplace equipment, tile, marble and the hand-crafted iron hardware throughout the estate. This company has been in business since 1827. Lamps and small bronzes were obtained from Tiffany.

Lucknow was equipped with the newest and very best technologies. A generator powered by the water of Shannon Brook provided electricity for the estate until community wide electrical power became available in 1921. Ammonia-brine refrigeration preserved food in two pantries and the basement. Western Electric's Inter-phones connected the entire building with several phones on each floor including servant areas and the stable and garage. This system was powered by dry cell batteries. Iron pipes were installed throughout the building for the central vacuum as well as iron conduits for the household wiring. Not only did the basement laundry include heated drying racks, but the butler's pantry had an electrically heated cabinet to warm the dinner plates.

Safety was also a concern. Tom had fire hydrants outside both the house and carriage house. Also, three were installed in the house. They were equipped with canvas hoses and bronze valves and were powered, as was the house plumbing, with water pressure from the spring with at least 70 pounds of pressure. His concern about lightning strikes and wildfires led him to build lookout towers on the peaks of the seven mountains.

There was an alarm system which monitored several of the first floor doors. The main rooms had call buttons to summon servants. The indicator panel for both was located in the servants hall.

Art

A painting by Alexander Pope, Jr. of "Sunshine," Plant's favorite horse, was installed in a place of honor above the mantle in the elegant dining room. Pope, a Boston artist who studied with William Copley and later studied anatomy with William Rimmer, an influential teacher of many Boston artists, specialized in animals and sporting birds.

Alphonse Jongers, a socially prominent Dutch painter born in France, captured Tom as a country squire gazing over his land. This

"Sunshine" Alexander Pope, Jr.

three quarter portrait may have been painted while Jongers lived and worked in Cass Gilbert's elegant building, 1917 Rodin Studios - 200 West 57th Street, New York City. In 1906, Jongers was given a large show at the Julius Oehme Art Galleries at 322 Fifth Avenue and 32nd Street with a dozen likenesses of men, women, and children. The review of the exhibition was very favorable.[243] Since the portrait study of Tom clearly reflects his New Hampshire property, it was painted sometime after 1911. (Note: the painting is on the frontispiece.)

The Plants admired Thomas Moran's paintings and purchased three canvases. One, "Zion Valley, South Utah" depicted the magnificence of the western lands; another was part of Moran's Venice series, "Lagoon Entrance To The Grand Canal, Venice" and the third was "Point Lobos, Monterey, California" currently part of the White House collection.

On the lakeside lawn, Tom and Olive had a small pond with a fountain. A bronze figure of a young boy with small wings sitting on a leaf and facing a frog spitting water was placed in the center. This joyful

"Sprite"

sculpture "Sprite" was designed by Lucy Currier Richards. Her iconic sculpture of "Putter Boy" was known to all the golfers who played the Pinehurst golf courses owned by the Plant's New Hampshire summer neighbors, Leonard and Gertrude Sise Tufts.

Tom was an admirer of Napoleon. In the living room there were four etchings of Napoleon and two bronze studies. At one time there was a limited edition set of red leather bound books in the living room — a history of Napoleon, perhaps a wedding gift from Olive.[244]

Tom and Olive took a break from their shopping in April 1914 and ventured to southern California for a stay of several days before arriving at the luxurious Palace Hotel in San Fransisco. Tom had family in the state, and the Dewey family frequently wintered in California. This trip would be a shared memory.

Tom and Olive had planned a comfortable home and had decorated it with elegant simplicity. They moved into their mountain home the fall of 1914. As winter approached they returned to New York and their home at the Gotham, enjoying museums, the theatre and opera, the city and business life.

Retirement Activities

The first issue of the *Daily Commercial Report* was released by the government on the first of January 1915. This was a daily publication of the Department of Commerce giving American businessmen pertinent industrial news. It printed all the business information received from embassies and consulates throughout the world. It also carried abstracts of investigations of the Department of Commerce in many commercial areas. When the discussion of a national press bureau for industrial news was first discussed, businessman Thomas Plant went on record favoring the plan.[245] Tom's views, advice and help were often sought by the business community.

His continuing concern for his family was demonstrated in an unusual way in January 1915. He was involved in yet another lawsuit — this time he was sued for $20,000 by William J. McGaffee, his longtime colleague in the Thomas G. Plant Shoe Company. McGaffee alleged Tom agreed to pay him this sum as he retired from the company in September 1910 if he would remain with the Plant Shoe Co. for two years under the control of the United Shoe Machinery Company. "McGaffee claims that the purpose of the agreement was to have him remain the superintendent of the company, so as to conserve and make more valuable the stock holdings of Plant's brother."[246] By agreement of the parties, judgement for the defendant with costs was entered in the United States District Court.

When the Lake Winnipesaukee Protective and Improvement Association met the end of July 1915 Tom Plant was elected vice-president. The membership of the organization was composed of businessmen from near-by towns and members of the summer colony. Many of the members were Massachusetts residents. His contributions were more than financial, he was willing to participate in the civic life of the community.[247] The Association had a number of committees that were involved in the conservation and protection of water quality, legislation, transportation, fisheries and the protection of property.

He was equally engaged in Bath, Maine. His friendships were life long and his family lived in the area. It was home. Bath held him in great esteem and the local newspapers followed his successes. He answered every request for money with a check —from $50 for the Naval Band concerts to $10,000 for the Red Cross in 1917.

OLIVE'S COMPANION

A new addition in the family arrived in the summer of 1915 and was Olive's constant companion. The pup's name has been lost in time, but this Eskie (American Eskimo) is found in many of the photographs that were taken of the property beginning in 1916 by the professional photographer, George Wesley Perry. A few snapshots were also taken by Tom.

The mouse is more interesting than the ball

In addition to Olive's Eskie, sheep and collies were brought to the estate. "Prize Sheep And Collies Arrive For Plant Farm" was the *Boston Herald* headline. "A consignment of blue ribbon sheep and two prize collie dogs, for the estate of Thomas G. Plant at Moultonboro, N.H. arrived in the Allan liner, *Sardinian,* Capt. McDonald, from Glasgow, said yesterday. The sheep will be used for breeding purposes."[248]

Now, this is very interesting!

Who needs collies?

A New Project

Olive returned to Toulon in May 1916 for a visit with her parents. In June she and Tom had a visit in Moultonborough from her brother, Maurice, after his graduation from Phillips Academy. It might be expected that they would see Maurice occasionally after he matriculated at Dartmouth in the fall of 1916. Olive made another visit to Toulon that fall. This was a pattern that repeated almost every year — at least one visit back to Illinois and occasional family trips back east to visit them.

Tom and Olive enjoyed traveling together, too. Trips were often made in the winter and we learned from Leander Pynn that they traveled to Japan in the winter of 1916[249] and the Breakers in Palm Beach in 1917. Olive maintained an album of their travels. Bermuda was visited in 1914, the Hawaiian Islands 1915, Nassau 1916, Cuba 1917, Yosemite in 1920 and undated visits to the Canadian Rockies.[250] Winter visits to the Salt River Valley area of Arizona began in 1920.[251]

To address the concerns of many who had been dismayed by the closing of Ossipee Park, Tom engaged his friend and neighbor, William O. Robinson, to start a livery business within the estate. Fred Ellis had constructed miles of roads throughout the property to provide access to the summits of the mountain peaks. A multiple-page brochure along with a map described the various drives with a price for each separate destination. The charges were based on the distance of each trip, but not by the hour. All the drivers were instructed to drive the horse drawn carriages slowly for the enjoyment of the visitors. The brochure included photographs of the Lucknow Estate, excluding the house and carriage house.[252] These were photographs that Tom had commissioned from George W. Perry, a Concord, New Hampshire photographer. An article about Tom's generosity in sharing the beauty of the mountain drives was sent to the *Boston Herald* by John F. Beebe of Meredith, New Hampshire, dated November 17, 1916.[253] In the rotogravure section of the *Boston Sunday Herald* in September 1917, a full page article with seven photographs was printed to tempt the visitor to return.[254]

Tom Plant had always been a man of 'big ideas' and tremendous energy. He was back in Bath for a few days to join a reunion of his school mates in the middle of October 1916. Two weeks later the Kennebec newspaper announced he'd bought the 24 acre Tarbox estate in Bath at the south end of Washington Street, known locally as Hospital Point. The property overlooked the Kennebec River with a scenic view along the banks of the river. His plan was to build an old folks home as a gift to the city of Bath. With this announcement came the notice that ground had already been broken for the foundation. His statement at the time relating to this gift was "It will be for old people who have no means of support." He further planned to endow the institution with a sum sufficient to meet every expense of operation.[255] The endowment amounted to around $400,000. The gift came as a happy surprise to everybody. Probably no one, until the announcement was made, ever dreamt of such a gift to Bath. Many only knew him as a favorite son who had succeeded beyond imagination as a manufacturer, but they knew he loved and supported his hometown generously.[256]

With a pace that was typical Plant, *The Bath Independent* announced on November 4 that Andrew S. Merrill had two steam drills, men and machinery ready to blast out the ledge for the large basement for the home. Penney & Nichols were awarded the contract for the concrete foundation and the architectural firm, Coolidge and Carlson of Boston, was working on the plans. "When these plans are completed, work will begin and will be carried on through the winter for a planned opening in the coming spring."[257] The next February, the first bill of the 78th State Legislature, signed by Speaker Bonney of Sagadahoc County, was a bill to incorporate the Old Folks' Home of Bath.[258]

Tom arrived in Bath in May 1917 to meet with his architect H. J. Carlson and Robert Logue of the Charles Logue Building Co. of Boston to view the progress being made in the construction. Again, he sought help from his friend, Scott R. Frye, to take charge of grading the grounds and building the roadways. It was expected the home would be ready for occupancy by the fall. The three and a half story Colonial Revival style building included a modern kitchen, elevator, telephones and automatic sprinklers on every floor. The rooms were spacious. Fireplaces were in the dining room and sun porch. Three verandas allowed the guests to oversee activity on the river. This was going to be a comfortable home for the elderly.

There were some objections to the naming of "Old Folks' Home" and a suggestion that "Long View Home" might be more acceptable. This had been the name of the Tarbox estate. However, the name remained the "Old Folks' Home" until Tom Plant's death in 1941. It is now known as the Plant Memorial Home which gives lasting recognition to its founder.

The Old Folks' Home — Bath, Maine

A plaque on the wall of the home expresses his vision:

"THIS HOME IS FOUNDED ON MY SINCERE BELIEF THAT THOSE WHO HAVE LIVED HONEST, INDUSTRIOUS LIVES AND ARE WITHOUT MEANS OR FRIENDS TO CARE FOR THEM, HAVE EARNED THE RIGHT TO BE CARED FOR. ONLY THROUGH THE LABOR AND EXPENDITURES OF OTHERS IS IT POSSIBLE FOR BUSINESS AND PROFESSIONAL MEN TO SUCCEED; THEREFORE IT IS THE DUTY OF THE STRONG AND SUCCESSFUL TO CARE FOR THE DESERVING, AGED POOR"

THOMAS G. PLANT

The officers of the new corporation were Dr. James Otis Lincoln, president; Walter S. Glidden and Frank B. Nichols, vice presidents; J. Edward Drake, treasurer; Frank H. Percy, secretary, and Edward B. Smith and Thomas G. Plant, Trustees.[259]

During the Christmas celebration in 1918, the residents paused to give thanks for the wonderful gift of their new home and expressed their deep gratitude to Thomas G. Plant for the privilege of living in such beautiful surroundings.[260]

Recreation

In February 1917, Tom visited the New York Boat Show in the Grand Central Palace and found a 6-cylinder boat to grace his new boat house. "He purchased a 32 foot Elco "V" express, which will go 30 mph."[261]

The New Boat House

"Motor Boating" International Magazine Company Vol. XIX June 1917

That wasn't the only boat Tom owned. He had commissioned the *Keen Kutter, a* 36' laker from the Goodhue and Hawkins boatyard located nearby in Wolfeboro. It was the longest laker ever built and was reportedly named for a leather-cutting machine developed by Plant. He wanted the fastest boat on the lake and it was. It is privately owned today and was exhibited in the Antique and Classic 43rd Annual Boat Show at the Wolfeboro Town Docks in 2016.

The Keen Kutter in 2016

Water sport activities included fly fishing in the mountain streams, trout fishing, swimming and canoeing on Shannon Pond. A tennis court was placed on a plateau between the house and the pond.

The fields and woods contained many varieties of game for the shooting enthusiast. Hunting parties were invited for the sport. A private nine-hole golf course completed the sporting activities on the estate.

Tom and Olive enjoyed riding together through the forty miles of roads on the estate and encouraged friends to join them.

Tom overlooks the mountain golf course, pond, and on the distant hill, his home, Lake Winnipesaukee and the Belknap Mountain range.

"The natural setting of the house with its background of lofty mountains, the immediate environment of rolling plateaus, shaded valleys, streams, and falls running through rocky gorges; the mile upon mile of wooded drives and bridle paths, and finally the far-flung vistas across a most beautiful lake off into the distance—provide a general assembling of natural beauty acknowledged by world wide travelers to be without equal."[262]

Tom and Olive enjoyed their home golf links. However, Tom began to envision a private club for golf on some of his extended acreage along the lakefront. They'd visited Pinehurst, North Carolina, perhaps encouraged by Leonard Tufts, developer of Pinehurst whose summer home was seven miles as the crow flies from Lucknow.

A Third Project

"Plant Building Finest Links In Whole Country" There it was, the headline[263] on August 7, 1919 announcing the golfing club Tom was building on 850 acres of his property that included some of his Winnipesaukee shore front. This property was first called The Oak Hill Development, then Bald Peak Country Club, Bald Peak Club Colony in 1927 and from 1932 on, Bald Peak Colony Club.

Olive Plant, in her letters describing the history of the Club to Elizabeth Crawford Wilkin,[264] depicts Clint Mason, a local who supervised the work at the site, as a man with a "get-along-with-it-now" attitude. Olive continues — "First the land had to be cleared, and this was a Herculean task for there was no heavy-duty machinery in those days, men with horses and dynamite must do the work. The trees were felled and hauled away, the stumps blasted as well as the rocks, and underneath the top layer of the latter there was often a second.

"Many of the workmen employed were those who had worked on the mountain property; Italians, teamsters and carpenters.

"While the golf course was being laid out [by] Mr. Plant and George Meredith, a professional from Pinehurst, with advice from Donald Ross, the well-known golf course architect, the building of the clubhouse and nine cottages went forward—six on the Ridge and three to the northeast of the clubhouse. There were also built a boathouse and a large dormitory-garage for about 20 cars and chauffeurs of the guests.

Dormitory/Garage at Bald Peak

"The clubhouse Mr. Plant built on the Browne Farm, the dormitory-garage on the Caverly Farm, and much of the Horne Farm became the 9th fairway and included the land running down to the lake of which Pine Point is now a part.

"When blasting a rock formation at the top of the hill which was eventually to be the 2nd Tee, a vein of quartz rock came to light rather like marble, very hard, shot through with light brown streaks. It proved to be decidedly decorative when the Italians used it for chimneys and pillars on the cottages, and for the dormers over the clubhouse entrance."

Olive continues in her letter to Elizabeth Wilkin to describe Tom's total involvement in the interior decoration of the clubhouse with the selection of fabrics, furniture, furnishings and fixtures. His same attention to detail extended to the nine cottages. Finally, two years after ground was broken, everything was finished and ready for guests.

Tom had invested several million dollars in the club and he expected a membership of people who shared his sense of decorum. He was described as totally absorbed in finding appropriate members and guests "who were vigorous, decorative, if possible, and who did things well." These attributes extended to women who rode gracefully and men who could shoot with a quick clear aim. He was looking for fit, congenial and attractive people who had a sense of style and purpose. As Olive described it— "Mr. Plant particularly wished the Club to be a colony of fine, genial and energetic people. Those who applied for membership were carefully screened. The membership was $2,500. Of course this was a deterrent to many but he considered it not too high for what was offered."

The Clubhouse

On August 31, 1920 in the Concord, New Hampshire law office of James W. Remick, the Club was incorporated. The Articles of Association tell us that "The property of the Corporation shall be evidenced by 200 certificates without par value, each representing 1/200th of said property, and each active member of the Club shall be entitled to one of the said certificates of ownership.

"At this meeting all the lands [5,588 acres] and all the buildings within the stipulated area including the Club Inn [Clubhouse], Garage, dormitories, 9 cottages and all other buildings in process of erection were conveyed by Mr. Plant to the Club 'in consideration of the 200 certificates of ownership.' "[265] By tying his personal estate to the Club he was able to add fly fishing, hunting and wonderful trails for hiking and equestrian pursuits to enhance the activities offered to the membership.

He was confident that his well planned Club with all of the amenities offered would sell itself. Unfortunately, this didn't prove to be true.

The Clubhouse With the Lucknow Estate In The Background

Seeking Members

Tom and Olive visited several of the top golf courses in New Hampshire to see exhibition matches and to play a round themselves. Bretton Woods and the Balsams were Donald Ross designed courses. Of course, these visits provided an opportunity to talk about his new club being built on such a spectacular site.

Transportation was another concern for prospective members. The Bald Peak Country Club seemed remote. This was either a blessing or a curse depending on your point of view. Fortunately, summer visitors to the mountains and lake area could come by train, then boat to nearby Center Harbor and Melvin Village. Automobile travel could be a little more difficult, although roads were being steadily improved. Tom played a role in their improvement at the National level. Gov. Bartlett named him a delegate to the annual meeting of the United States Good Roads Association meeting in Hot Springs, Arkansas.[266] An airplane flying field and hanger were also being planned for the use of Club members as well as hydro-airplane service.[267]

The Club's opening was scheduled for August 1, 1921. Tom's position on the initial Board of Directors was Treasurer. He was authorized to borrow $300,000 to complete the final finishes on the construction projects by the opening day. He came back to the Board with success in finding only $60,000. Tom provided the remaining $240,000. Now, it become even more important to find members. He was discomforted by the fact that he'd only found eight people who were willing to invest $2,500 in this beautiful club on which he'd devoted three years of his life and contributed an enormous amount of money.

Tom knew the value of the printed word. He arranged for publicity — newspaper articles, and an illustrated brochure that described the Club and golf course features. He also arranged an exhibition match between the touring British pro golfers Sandy Herd and J. H. Taylor, (both winners of the British Open) and the Massachusetts amateur golf champions, Francis Ouimet and Jesse Guilford. "This is the first match to be played at Tom Plant's new $2,000,000 golf club, the Bald Peak Country Club, one of the most exclusive clubs in the country."[268] The exhibition brought a number of golfing enthusiasts, several of whom became members. Among the spectators was Percy D. Haughton, Harvard Football All-American, later Harvard's head football coach whose winning record brought the team to four National Football Championships in 1908, 1910, 1912 and 1913. In 1916 he became the President and part owner of the Boston National League Baseball Club, the Braves.[269] He was a well-known and well respected member of the athletic community and a first class golfer. He made an extended trip on Bald Peak's behalf to interest clubmen in other cities. Slowly the membership grew with members joining not only from the Boston area, but New York, Philadelphia, St. Louis and other western cities.

Although Tom was certain the Club would succeed, he reaccessed his financial contributions to the Club and proposed to the Executive Committee in a letter dated November 11, 1922 "that the Club return to him the nine completed and furnished cottages situated on the hill near the clubhouse and the lots on which they were built together with all the other real estate and buildings now belonging to the Club comprising more than 5,000 acres…and being the same conveyed by him to the Club…on December 4, 1920 excepting that portion of the property…needed for the usual purposes of a country club…in consideration of the cancellation by him of all his claims against the Club on account of his personal services and of the assumption by him of all outstanding obligations against the Club of whatsoever nature. (All this amounted to more than $260,000)."[270] His proposal was unanimously accepted. He also proposed to set up a newly formed Bald Peak Realty Company to lease all the Club lands and buildings with the exception of his nine cottages and the land they stood on and all the potential house lots back to the membership with the assumption that there would be 200 members making annual payments of $200. for a total of $200,000. Tom would be the Treasurer.

In December 1921, Tom became one of the leading spirits and backer of Mid-Pines, a private club and the newest and most scenic of the Pinehurst, North Carolina golf courses developed by his friend and summer neighbor, Leonard Tufts.[271] Tufts returned the favor by joining Bald Peak. Perhaps conversations between these two men led to Tufts belief revealed in an article written for *The Pilot* (Pinehurst's newsletter) by Richard J. (Pete) Moss in the June 12, 2014 issue that "for Pinehurst to work, Leonard thought of it as having two parts. The first part was in the general operation that included the hotels, the golf courses and other amenities. He believed that you could do no better than break even on this part of the business. The profit would come from the second part: 'associated activities' such as selling real estate, building homes and selling services to an established clientele."

For the next few years, Tom controlled the Bald Peak Board of Directors with Olive, his brother William, Frederick L. Emery, his attorney and friend, and Elbert H. Brock. The membership increased with new members from Pittsburgh, Pennsylvania; Montclair, New

Jersey; Waterville, Maine; Brattleboro, Vermont and Greenwich, Connecticut.

In January 1925 a new Board of Directors was elected with four members of the Club and Thomas Plant, Treasurer. By the fall, Tom Plant proposed the Club purchase eight of his cottages for around $250,000 but the Board didn't make the commitment. There was a continuing need for operations funding and until there was full membership, funds still needed to be borrowed. Tom guaranteed he would cover operating deficits for the years 1925 and 1926. When he offered his resignation from the Board the end of 1927 it was accepted with regret.

Later in 1929 he offered his remaining 65 membership shares to the Club for the reduced price of $2,250. Elizabeth Crawford Wilkins sums up her review of the Club minutes, "So, in effect, on that day (November 1, 1929) Mr. Plant sold his rights to the Club for $146,250 with the exception of the (now) six cottages." [272]

The Final Years

Tom circa 1927

The financial burden continued and in typical Tom Plant fashion slick ads were placed in magazines and newspapers to offer his home for sale. The first ad was placed in *Country Life* magazine in the October 1924 issue. The ad included seventeen pages of description of the property and George W. Perry's photographs of the Lucknow Estate and model farm, Bald Peak Club Colony and his brother's lake property. A brochure was printed around the same time and included the same information.

In August 1927, another ad was placed in Boston, Chicago, and New York newspapers in their Sunday Rotogravure sections,

"For Sale A Mountain and Lake Estate — Six Thousand Three Hundred Acres." Another brochure was available for this offering, too.

By the spring and summer of 1928, the ad was reworked,

"The Wise Man of Wealth Over Fifty Adds Years to His Life by Having an Interesting, Healthful and Profitable Outdoor Occupation." The ads were sent to Cleveland, Pittsburgh, Detroit, St Louis, Los Angeles, New York and Boston. This time the brochure was accompanied by a letter…

LUCKNOW
MOULTONBORO, N. H.

Dear Sir:

Possibly you may be interested in a summer home for the family, a place where young people can find healthful, normal outdoor attractions of every nature, far removed from all disturbing elements.

For a man of wealth with a family who enjoy all varieties of outdoor sports and are lovers of horses, "Lucknow" is, without qualification, the most livable and attractive mountain estate in America.

This estate should be owned by one who is intensely human, a lover of nature in its grandeur, and with such breadth of thought as to require wide vistas of mountains and waters to interest, rest and satisfy the mind. "Lucknow" owned by such a one would be maintained in its present beauty and passed on to coming generations.

It is necessary for one to visit this place to realize that the pictures and descriptions given in the book are totally inadequate to convey the exceeding beauty and extensiveness of this property. Visitors to "Lucknow" are of one opinion,—that they have never seen a more beautiful spot in any part of the world.

Trusting that this book may be of interest to you, I remain

Very truly yours,

THOMAS G. PLANT, *Owner*

The estate was not sold. Tom and Olive remained at Lucknow. Friends and family enjoyed visiting them. The Bald Peak community enjoyed seeing them, playing golf with them and hearing Tom's stories about his life. An invitation to Lucknow to have tea with Olive was a treasured experience. An invitation to fish for trout in Shannon Brook with Tom, another treat. It's unknown how much was known about their dwindling financial situation. They might have shared stories about the losses in Russian bonds and the "stock market crash." The Great Depression affected many. Tom Plant resigned from the Club around 1935, but his resignation was not accepted and the Board made both Thomas and Olive Plant Life Members of Bald Peak. It would have been understood by the members that the construction of the Bald Peak Club had put them in straightened circumstances.

A mountain car that had been built locally for the Plants by Leander Pynn using an elongated 1928-1929 Ford chassis [273] was now used to show potential buyers as well as friends around the estate

Mountain Car

Olive shares a glimpse of her life in her Wellesley Class Notes: In 1930 she paints a picture of the scenic beauty of their part of New Hampshire. Her gardens and greenhouse provide pleasure. She enjoys watching the wild animals that have become tame, feeding the birds, and working in her greenhouse. She drives her own car and does her own shopping. She describes a quiet life. They were traveling less and had begun to spend the New England winters at Lucknow where they snow shoed and skied and even had a toboggan run built on the property. She does share that she and Tom had recently discovered Chandler, Arizona in the Salt River Valley as having a winter climate they found delightful. Every five years when her class notes are reported, she promises to attend reunion, but she never does.

Tom's business and personal successes had made him a celebrity. He had been in the headlines all around the country, especially after Caroline divorced him. That had made it difficult for Tom and Olive to have a private life. But now that was changing. Olive and Tom were both quiet and reserved. They had similar interests and the time to enjoy the social life at Bald Peak and the beauty of the lakes and mountains that surrounded Lucknow.

Tom remained a trustee of the Old Folks' Home in Bath and looked forward to seeing his friends who served on the Board with him. Following a meeting in November 1933 he met with his friend, Capt. S. R. Percy, the president of the Board, along with several of the trustees in the directors room of the Bath Trust Company. "He expressed himself much gratified by the fine condition of the home and its management. He told the trustees more about his objective in establishing it…he modestly but feelingly expressed his pleasure in being able to help so many of his old townsmen in their last days."[274]

A personal loss was the unexpected death of his brother in April 1934.[275] William F. Plant had been visiting Tom and Olive at Lucknow and had a fatal heart attack while there. William and his family had moved from New Hampshire to California following the demise of Plant Brothers Shoe Company. He was a widower, his wife Margaret having died a few years earlier.

Bath, Maine honored the benefactors of the 'Shipping City'

with a front page group of photographs in *The Bath Independent* on July 22, 1937. Tom's was front and center.

Bath hadn't been the only community to receive financial support from Tom. The Boston newspapers often publicized his substantial gifts to organizations. He was interested in helping improve life for the community and he had been very generous.

Loans and Mortgages

In December 1928 Tom and Olive began mortgaging their property. Robert Clayton of Boston, held a mortgage for a period of ten months when it was reassigned to Joseph H. Emery. Emery was a friend of the Plants and was also a member of Bald Peak. The mortgage was for $150,000. In time Emery would purchase three of Tom's Bald Peak cottages.[276]

In the 1937 tax levy for the town of Moultonborough, Thomas G. Plant was in arrears for taxes amounting to $5,349.48 on 6,635 acres. He made arrangements with his first wife, Caroline Griggs Plant to convey a property in Tuftonboro to her on January 11, 1937.[277] On September 20, 1938, Caroline conveys the property back.[278] Presumably the financial arrangements between them allowed him to pay his taxes. In 1941, a lawsuit was filed against the Joseph Emery estate by Caroline Griggs Plant for her rights in Plant mortgages.[279] Apparently the property swap was actually another mortgage. This must have been a very difficult path for both Olive and Tom to take.

It appears that he was also able to obtain a mortgage from the Old Folks' Home on August 15, 1939.[280] This, too, would have been difficult, but the Bath Trust Company acting as trustee had cautiously but wisely invested the large endowment Tom had given to the Home. It might be expected that the trustees would have voted to help Tom.

There was an asset on the property that could have given some financial relief. The mountain had an abundance of large trees that had monetary value. Fred Tobey, an area lumberman and Tom Plant's friend, offered to buy the logging rights to the forest, which he estimated would be worth $750,000.[281] Tom couldn't bring himself to sign a contract with Tobey. However, the Hurricane of 1938 did what Tom couldn't bring himself to do. This massive storm brought millions of trees down and caused damage to homes and businesses as it tore through New England. Tom hurried to New York to broker some of his lumber, but the large numbers of felled trees throughout New England caused the government to set up a single agency to salvage the lumber - The Northeast Timber Salvage Administration (NETSA). It would control the market.

In September 1940 the attorney for Joseph Emery paid the Moultonborough taxes for Tom in the amount $6,635.97. This action protected Emery's investment.[282]

Tom was known for paying his workers, but perhaps delaying his tax payments. The farm was supplying food for them and providing for the Club. The 1940 United States census lists Robert G. Patterson as caretaker of the Plant estate and Clarence Frye, caretaker of the farm. Food and comfortable housing were the benefits of working for the Plants.

Some of the estate staff shown in the 1930 census were no longer listed. Martina Malmquist, listed as "servant" but probably the housekeeper, was gone by 1940.

1940 - 1941

Olive writes to her family in June 1940 that she wouldn't be driving back home to Illinois with her brother, Maurice and nephew, John. She explains their "affairs seem to be reaching a crisis." Maurice had come to New Hampshire for his 20th Dartmouth reunion and brought John along with him to see the college he would be entering in the fall. This was John's first visit to Lucknow. The mountains and streams offered any number of areas to explore. Tom gave John a .22 rifle and taught him to shoot. In their later years both John and his brother Phelps tried to describe the most elegant hand-made gun they'd ever seen.[283] It had been elaborately carved and engraved. Olive writes a newsy letter to her parents describing the visit and how her nephew John entertained himself and helped her with various chores. Their visit brought a welcome respite.

She says no more about the crisis, but it was well understood that Tom was broke, and the juggling to stay afloat was difficult.

It had become obvious by now that their financial situation would not and could not improve. They were now totally financially dependent on family and friends. Olive told her brother that the size of the project to build and furnish the club had been too large a commitment to take on after building Lucknow and the Old Folks' Home. A country club with a congenial group of friends would provide a way of life that he wanted for Olive and himself. He had a great deal of confidence in his ability to make it work. He had always worked very hard, but this time the wind was out of his sails.

On March 2, 1941, Joseph H. Emery died. Tom and Olive knew it was only a matter of time until the mortgage would be foreclosed — the financial balancing act ended.

Tom entered the local hospital in Laconia to have major surgery in July. He failed to rally and died after four days in hospital on July 25, 1941.[284] Mary Case, Olive and Tom's good friend and one of the first families of Bald Peak Colony Club, wrote the moving tribute that begins this book.

The accolades began…brilliance and dash, shrewd businessman, philanthropist. Avid reader, student of history — particular interest in Napoleon. Courtly around women, low cultured voice, impeccably tailored in fine materials. Quiet, reserved, interesting.

Olive Dewey Plant

Olive's brother Mills and his wife, Irene, came east for the memorial service and stayed to help Olive pack her personal belongings to ship back to Toulon which now would be her home.

Her life in Moultonborough was at an end. She, with help from Mills, would handle her administratrix duties for the estate from Toulon or from California when she visited her brother Phil and her parents who were now wintering in Pasadena.

Her 86 year old father, Charles P. Dewey, died in October 1943. At the time of his retirement as President of the Bank in 1938, he "had been active for over 61 years and had the longest period of continuous service of any business man in the city. Such was the respect the community held for him, Toulon stores and business houses were closed during the funeral service."[285]

Olive and her mother continued spending the winters in California until Mrs. Dewey's health prevented her from traveling. She died in the summer of 1956.

Although Olive enjoyed her brother Maurice's large family who lived only eight miles away in Galva, Illinois, she was persuaded by her brother Phil to move to California where he was living. She moved to Pasadena in 1961.

Her niece and nephews, who got to know Olive after her return to Toulon, have warm memories of her. Her niece, Maurice's daughter Judy, describes Olive as being reserved and somewhat stoic. "I realized she was much like my father, quiet and undemonstrative, but actually kind and loving."

Phil Dewey, Judith Dewey Newell & Olive Dewey Plant July 1960

She remembers her Aunt Olive's good taste and her interest in the theater and opera, museums and travel. Olive loved nature and enjoyed watching the birds and small animals in the open fields beyond the family home in Toulon. In fact, there was a large window in the living room in her grandparents home that may have prompted Olive's wish for a similar one in her living room at Lucknow.

In 1968 Olive purchased a home in Leisure World, Laguna Hills ,California and was cared for there by a nurse companion, Nanlee Palmer, the widow of a doctor. Olive apparently left her home to Mrs. Palmer who was still living there a number of years after Olive's death on November 17, 1976. Olive was 93 years old.

Olive Dewey Plant in 1967, age 84

Lucknow “Castle In the Clouds”

The Plant Memorial Home, Bath, Maine

Bald Peak Colony Club, Moultonborough, NH

ACKNOWLEDGEMENTS

Ann Hackl, as Chair of The Lakes Region Conservation Trust (LRCT) played a significant role in raising the $5,900,000 for the LRCT to purchase in 2002 the 5,500 acre Castle in the Clouds. In 2006, the Castle Preservation Society (CPS) was created, with Ann as its founding Chair and chief fundraiser, to take over the management of the Castle in the Clouds business and the restoration of the historic buildings and their grounds on 135 operational acres. Ann continues to head CPS's fundraising which over the last 15 years has restored and transformed about three quarters of the estate. I am indebted to Ann for sharing with me her interviews with the estate architect's grandsons which provided insights into the construction process and Tom Plant's personality. Above all, I am grateful to Ann for her suggestions and enthusiastic support for this book.

Penelope Hartshorne Batcheler, now deceased, a retired National Park Service Historical Architect and Sandwich, NH summer resident, greatly helped CPS's initial understanding of the restoration task ahead. Her introduction to her nephews, Tom and Phil Beal, provided CPS with first hand reminiscences about construction plans, materials sources, and Plant's interactions with his architect, their grandfather, J. Williams Beal. It was Penny Batcheler's research that initially identified Beal as Lucknow's architect and her research that located in the Hanover, MA Historical Society Beal's wife's diary, filled with interesting details about her husband and Plant.

Nancy Gaver was the museum manager of the Plant's home, Lucknow and gathered and shared early brochures and guide training materials. Her research and resources added a great deal of background.

Bruce Reynolds of nearby Meredith, NH shared his grandfather's photographs of the construction crews. They were part of the large body of special skilled carpenters who worked on all the buildings and designed the beautiful floor patterns in the octagonal rooms in Lucknow.

Olive Plant's niece and nephews, children of her brother Maurice, were very helpful in describing their Aunt Olive. Through telephone conversations they gave me a picture of a private, reserved and warm woman. John Dewey sent the photograph of Marilla and Olive.

Judy Dewey Newell also shared family photographs and Olive's albums as well as excerpts from albums that showed some of Tom and Olive's travels. Our conversations were so helpful to me in understanding Olive's ability to cope with the challenging situation she found herself in the last few years of her marriage.

Robin A. S. Haynes, of the Patten Free Library's Sagadahoc History Room in Bath, Maine directed me to resource material that was part of its collection of material about Tom Plant, a favorite son of the community.

Paula Herson, Vice President of the Plant Memorial Home Board also offered information about the Plant Memorial Home's collection of Thomas Plant artifacts, gifts from his widow, Olive Dewey Plant.

The American Antiquarian Society's newspaper collection has been invaluable in providing contemporary reports of events. Reading the news of the day added "color" and continuity to the story.

Wonderfully helpful support and encouragement was given by my family. My daughters, Marion Radin and Mary Hagan, were filled with suggestions and provided thorough editing.

I thank my most loving and supportive husband, Elliot, for his guidance, encouragement, editing, and technical support throughout the development of this book. I believe that he has enjoyed this project as much as I have.

NOTES

[1] United States Passport Application December 30, 1893 Boston

[2] *History of Bath and Environs, Sagadahoc Co., Maine 1607-1894* by Parker McCobb Reed, 1894

[3] Supreme Judicial Court, Sagadahoc County, Bath, Maine v. 18, Petition No 2-382A, ca 1787-1906

[4] Registry of Deeds, Church Records, Sagadahoc County, Bath, Maine

[5] Federal Naturalization Records, August 19, 1882

[6] *History of Bath, Maine* by Henry Wilson Owen, Bath, Maine, 1916

[7] Lorraine Boissoneault, smithsonian.com January 26, 2017

[8] *The Bath Independent,* Bath, Maine April 21, 1949, p. 1

[9] Sagadahoc County, Maine Registry of Deeds

[10] ibid.

[11] Sagadahoc County, Maine Death Record # 72, date of death June 30, 1895, age 87 years, 3 months. This date indicates a birth year, 1808

[12] Nancy Lovas, Business Reference and Research Specialist for Library of Congress, August 2017

[13] City of Bath, Maine Comprehensive Action Plan, 2009

[14] "World's Greatest Shoe Manufacturer" *The Bath Independent* Bath, Maine June 4, 1910, pages 1, 2

[15] *The Shoe Industry* Frederick J. Allen, Henry Holt & Co. New York, 1922

[16] "Shoe Industry Notable Dead" *The Boston Herald,* Boston, Massachusetts July 26, 1941, p. 7

[17] Maine Historical Society "Ice: A Maine Commodity"

[18] U. S. Civil War Draft Registration Records, Bath, Sagahadoc County, Maine June, 1863

[19] Public Documents of Maine: Annual Reports for the Year 1878

[20] 1880 US Federal Census; Lynn, Massachusetts

[21] Census Reports, Vol. IX, 12th Census of US, 1900, Manufacturers, Part III

[22] *The Bath Independent,* Bath, Maine July 31, 1941, p. 4

[23] "Thomas G. Plant an Expert Skater" *The Shoe Retailer* Boston, Massachusetts January 2, 1900

[24] Bath Historical Society "Notes about the man, Thomas Gustave Plant"

[25] *Bath Daily Times,* Bath, Maine September 1, 1921, p. 3

[26] *Northern Sandlots, A Social History of Maritime Baseball* Colin D. Howell

[27] "Retires With Millions, Wife Sues For Divorce" *Syracuse Herald,* Syracuse, New York January 23, 1911. p. 4

[28] ibid.

[29] Lynn, Massachusetts City Directory, 1888

[30] Marriages Registered in the City of Lynn for the year 1886, p. 271

[31] Lynn, Massachusetts City Directory, 1892

[32] "A History of the Shoe and Leather Industries of the United States" Vol. II by Charles H. McDermott, Boston, John W. Deneny & Company Boston, 1920

[33] ibid.

[34] *Boston Daily Advertiser*, December 26, 1892, p. 6

[35] Queen Quality Sales Brochure, circa 1900

[36] Board of Arbitration, Public Documents of Massachusetts,
Vol II, 1893

[37] "Shoe Strike in Lynn" *Boston Herald,* Boston, Massachusetts September 20, 1893, p. 5

[38] "Prefer Work to Want" *Boston Herald*, Boston, Massachusetts December 18, 1893, p. 5

[39] "Retires With Millions" *Syracuse Herald*, Syracuse, New York January 23, 1911, p. 4

[40] "Wedding Days" *Boston Journal* Boston, Massachusetts June 27, 1895, p. 5

[41] "Plant-Griggs" T*he Daily Inter Ocean,* Chicago, Illinois June 27, 1895, p. 8

[42] "Biographical Sketches of the Leading Men of Chicago" Chicago, Wilson and St. Clair, Publishers, 1868

[43] "S. C. Griggs Dies from Paralysis" *Chicago Tribune* April 6, 1897, p. 12

[44] *Appleton's Cyclopedia of American Biography, Vol, II* James Grant Wilson & John Fiske, editors, New York: D. Appleton & Co. 1888

[45] "Samuel C. Griggs, Jr." *Chicago Tribune,* Chicago, Illinois January 13, 1890, p. 3

[46] Adam Schutzman, Archives Librarian, Lasell College. Newton, MA 2019

[47] "Grain, Once Scattered" Rambles on the History of St. Paul's Church, Albany, New York George William Warren. April 23, 2015

[48] "The Chicago Blue Book, 1894" The Chicago Directory Company 1894

[49] "A New Feature in Society" *Chicago Tribune* Chicago, Illinois February 17, 1889, p. 14

[50] "Dimple and Dumplings" *Daily Inter Ocean* Chicago, Illinois March 8, 1891, p. 25

[51] Board of Arbitration, Public Documents of Massachusetts, Vol. II, 1895

[52] "Victory for Strikers in Thomas G. Plant's Factory Settled" *Boston Journal* Boston, Massachusetts October 16, 1895, p. 2

[53] "Labor Unions Cause Assigned for Purposed Transfer to West of a Lynn Concern" *Boston Journal* Boston, Massachusetts December 31, 1895, p. 5

[54] The Herter Brothers Archives Winterthur Museum Library Centreville, Delaware

[55] "Herter Brothers" William Hosley *American Heritage* 1995, Vol. 46

[56] "Personal" *Daily Inter Ocean* Chicago, Illinois December 29, 1895, p. 26

[57] "Social Life" *Boston Herald,* Boston, Massachusetts April 5, 1896, p. 27

[58] Suffolk County Registry of Deeds, Vol. 152. June 8, 1896

[59] "The Plant Side" *Boston Daily Advertiser* Boston, Massachusetts August 4, 1896, p. 2

[60] "Injunction Granted" *Boston Journal* Boston, Massachusetts. August 15, 1896, p. 1

[61] "Claim Victory" *Boston Post* Boston, Massachusetts September 6, 1896, p. 2

[62] "Strike Practically Ended" *Boston Herald* Boston, Massachusetts September 6, 1896, p. 6

[63] "Satisfied Now" *Boston Journal* Boston, Massachusetts November 20, 1896, p. 3

[64] Suffolk County Registry of Deeds, Vol. 188. January 14, 1897

[65] Suffolk County Registry of Deeds, Vol. 152 January 14, 1897

[66] "Publisher Griggs Dead" *Emporia Gazette* Emporia, Kansas. April 6, 1897, p. 1

[67] Sharon Historic and Cultural Resources Survey Project, undated

[68] "Mrs. Sophia Plant" *The Bath Independent* May 13, 1899, p. 4

[69] "A Brilliant Season Opens at Manchester-by-the Sea" *Boston Herald* Boston, Massachusetts July 2, 1899, p. 27

[70] "Many Guests at Rangeley" *Boston Herald* Boston, Massachusetts June 10, 1900, p. 14

[71] "Gilded Age of Manchester-by-the-Sea" Publication of the Manchester Historical Museum

[72] *"Social Life" Boston Herald* Boston, Massachusetts. July 14, 1901, p. 32

[73] "An Afternoon Concert" *Boston Herald* Boston, Massachusetts January 7, 1902, p. 8

[74] *San Francisco Chronicle* San Francisco, California April 11, 1902, p. 6

[75] "Many Voyagers to Europe" *Boston Herald* Boston, Massachusetts June 24, 1902, p. 11

[76] "Manchester-By-The-Sea" *Boston Herald* Boston, Massachusetts. August 23, 1903, p. 27

[77] "Social Notes" *Boston Herald* Boston, Massachusetts April 10, 1904, p. 27

[78] "Social Notes" *Boston Herald* Boston, Massachusetts July 28, 1903, p. 31

[79] "Labor Problem" *Lexington Leader* Lexington, Kentucky November 23, 1903, p. 4

[80] "Where Work Is A Pleasure" *Boston Herald* Boston, Massachusetts September 20, 1903, p. 13

[81] "Shoe Employees Dance" *Boston Herald* Boston, Massachusetts April 19, 1904, p. 35

[82] "Two Bath Boys" *Bath Daily Times* Bath, Maine April 25, 1902

[83] "In Advance of the Times" *Boot and Shoe Recorder* Boston, Massachusetts September 18, 1901

[84] Olmsted Archives Job # 03792

[85] "For Use Of Employees" *Boston Globe* Boston, Massachusetts May 28, 1910, p. 8

[86] See note: 14

[87] ibid.

[88] ibid.

[89] "Industrial Combinations" *New York Tribune* New York, New York February 11, 1899, p. 14

[90] "A Shoe Machinery Trust" *The New York Times* New York, New York July 19, 1899, p. 7

[91] "Shoemakers' Convention" *Dallas Morning News* Dallas, Texas August 10, 1899, p. 4

[92] "News from the Field of Capital" *Daily People* New York, New York July 20, 1901, p. 4

[93] "Re-Organization in Shoe Machinery" *Boot and Shoe Recorder, v. 39* Boston, Massachusetts July - September 1901

[94] "Queen Quality Shoes" *Naugatuck Daily News* Naugatuck Connecticut November 30, 1901, p. 3

[95] "In and About the Courts" *Boston Herald* Boston, Massachusetts. December 12, 1901, p. 11

[96] "To the Women of America" *Lima News* Lima, Ohio October 3, 1902, p. 2

[97] "Thomas G. Plant adds Comet to his Stable" *Worcester Daily Spy* Worcester, Massachusetts August 13, 1903, p. 3

[98] "Good Races at Readville" *The Boston Globe* Boston, Massachusetts August 13, 1903, p. 3

[99] "Seven Races Decided" *The Boston Globe* Boston, Massachusetts October 8, 1903, p. 3

[100] "Table Gossip" *The Boston Globe* Boston, Massachusetts November 22, 1903, p. 42

[101] "New Quarters Of the Gentlemen's Driving Club" *The Boston Globe* Boston, Massachusetts January 7, 1904, p. 9

[102] "Mrs. T. G. Plant Stops Speedway Runaway" *Boston Post* Boston, Massachusetts January 19, 1904, p. 5

[103] "Social Life" *Boston Herald* Boston, Massachusetts May 07, 1905, p. 35

[104] "Horse Show In The South" *New York Times* New York, New York April 28, 1905

[105] "Society Attends Open Air Horse Show" *Boston Herald* Boston, Massachusetts May 24, 1905, p. 10

[106] "Social Life" *Boston Herald* Boston, Massachusetts October 22, 1905, p. 34

[107] "Plants Make Sweep In Harness Classes" *Boston Herald* Boston, Massachusetts May 23, 1908, p. 8

[108] "Will Appeal to President" *Boston Herald* Boston, Massachusetts October 5, 1905, p. 8

[109] "Strike Blow At Leather Trust" *Boston Herald* Boston, Massachusetts January 23, 1906, p. 4

[110] "State Street Chat" *Boston Herald* January 15, 1907, p. 11

[111] "Want Winthrop Street Site for School" *Boston Herald* Boston, Massachusetts May 9, 1907, p. 5

[112] "Real Estate Exchange" *Boston Herald* Boston, Massachusetts May 15, 1907, p. 12

[113] "Selling Insurance At Savings Banks" *Augusta Chronicle* Augusta, Georgia. August 18, 1907, p. 5

[114] "Donate Many Autos for Children's Run" *Boston Herald* Boston, Massachusetts July 26, 1906, p. 14

[115] "Vanderbilt Four First in London" *New York Times* New York, New York June 7, 1907, p. 25

[116] "Bangor Bench Show Attracting Specials" *Boston Herald* Boston, Massachusetts July 29, 1909, p. 24

[117] "New England Kennel Club" *Boston Herald* Boston, Massachusetts February 25, 1910, p. 5

[118] "From The Field Of Capital" *Daily People* New York, New York March 10, 1906, p. 3

[119] "Shoe Machinery Combine Planned" *Boston Herald* Boston, Massachusetts March 9, 1906, p. 1

[120] ibid.

[121] "Shoe Machinery Trust Wins" *Springfield Republican* Springfield, Massachusetts May 25, 1906, p. 6

[122] "Text of the Shoe Lease" *Boston Herald* Boston, Massachusetts September 28, 1910, p. 1

[123] "Shoe Machine Men To Continue Fight" *Boston Herald* Boston, Massachusetts February 2, 1908, p. 14

[124] "Plant Plans Shoe Machinery War" *Boston Herald* Boston, Massachusetts January 6, 1910, p. 1

[125] ibid.

[126] "Plant Company Issues A Statement" *Boston Globe* Boston, Massachusetts January 13, 1907, p. 4

[127] Correspondence with Tate Billings who lived in this space in the 1970's when the buildings were used as an artist colony

[128] Author's personal conversation with Tate Billings, an artist who lived in this space in the 1970's

[129] "Retires with Millions" *Syracuse Herald* Syracuse, New York January 23, 1911, p. 4

[130] "Thomas G. Plant's Machinery Announcements" *Boot and Shoe Recorder* Boston, Massachusetts June 8, 1910

[131] "Plant to Build Shoe Machinery" *Boston Herald* Boston, Massachusetts June 7, 1910, p. 14

[132] Wonder Worker Shoe Machinery Ad *Boston Herald* Boston, Massachusetts July 12, 1910, p. 10

[133] "Plant May War On United Shoe" *Boston Herald* Boston, Massachusetts March 1, 1910, p. 1

[134] "Facts about the Situation in Shoe Machinery" *Boston Herald* Boston, Massachusetts July 7, 1910, p. 12

[135] "United Shoe Opens Campaign Against Thomas G. Plant" *Boston Journal* Boston, Massachusetts July 8, 1910, p. 1

[136] "Shoe Machinery Co. Sues" *The New York Times* New York, New York July 8, 1910, p. 4

[137] "Is the United Shoe Machinery Company An Illegal Trust & Monopoly?" *Boston Journal* Boston, Massachusetts July 8, 1910, p. 12

[138] "Mr. Chas.H. Jones, Pres. Commonwealth Shoe & Leather Co" *Boston Herald* Boston, Massachusetts July 13, 1910, p. 8

[139] "Plant Litigation Ended?" *Springfield Republican* Springfield, Massachusetts September 24, 1910, p. 16

[140] "Suit Filed Against 'Wonder Worker' Machinery" *Boot and Shoe Recorder* Boston, Massachusetts August 3, 1910

[141] "Plant Answers United Shoe" *Boston Herald* Boston, Massachusetts August 11, 1910, p. 5

[142] "New Incorporations" *Boot and Shoe Recorder* Boston, Massachusetts September 14, 1910

[143] "Plant May War on United Shoe" *Boston Herald* Boston, Massachusetts March 1, 1910, p. 1

[144] "500 Discharged In Plant Shops" *Boston Herald* Boston, Massachusetts September 25, 1910, p. 9

[145] "Plant's Project Nursed By Rival" *Boston Herald* Boston, Massachusetts September 28, 1910, p. 1

[146] "Plant Loses $300,000 Suit" *Boston Herald* Boston, Massachusetts May 2, 1912, p. 3

[147] "Denies Barring Plant Loans" *Boston Herald* Boston, Massachusetts December 12, 1913 p. 9

[148] "That Plant Deal" *Bath Independent* Bath, Maine October 8, 1910, p. 1

[149] "Decides Against Plant" *Fitchburg Daily Sentinel* Fitchburg, Massachusetts May 3, 1913, p. 12

[150] "Gives $100,000 Now" *Boston Globe* Boston, Massachusetts December 29, 1910, p. 8

[151] "Monopoly Is Seen In Shoe Machinery" *New York Times* New York, New York July 27, 1911, p. 10

[152] "Shoe Machinery Men Indicted in Boston" *New York Times* New York, New York September 20, 1911, p. 6

[153] "Heads of Shoe Machinery Co. Are Indicted" *Boston Herald* Boston, Massachusetts September 20, 1911, p. 1

[154] "Begins Suit to Dissolve Shoe Machinery Company" *Springfield Daily News* Springfield, Massachusetts December 13, 1911, p. 5

[155] "Brandeis Talks About Monopolies" *Springfield Union* Springfield, Massachusetts October 3, 1912, p. 4

[156] "French Pleased At Shoe Ruling" *Boston Herald* Boston, Massachusetts March 4, 1912, p. 5

[157] "Says Shoe Company Used Pressure" *Boston Herald* Boston, Massachusetts June 13, 1913, p. 10

[158] United States v. United Shoe Machinery Corp., 391 U.S. 244 (1968)

[159] "Wife of Thomas G. Plant Gets Divorce Decree After Hearing" *Boston Herald* Boston, Massachusetts October 29, 1912, p. 3

[160] "Rally To Support Of Miss Haberley" *Boston, Journal* Boston, Massachusetts February 13, 1911, p. 5

[161] "Whitney Horse Show Opened" *Boston Herald* Boston, Massachusetts September 10, 1910, p. 7

[162] "T. G. Plant Sued By Wife" *New York Times* New York, New York January 20, 1911 p. 1

[163] "Court Record For The Day" *Boston Herald* Boston, Massachusetts March 13, 1913, p. 14

[164] "Suing Shoe King Mrs. Plant Accuses Unknown Woman" *Boston Journal* Boston, Massachusetts. January 20, 1911, p. 1

[165] "Plant Loses $300,000 Suit" *Boston Herald* Boston, Massachusetts October 5. 1910 p. 3

[166] See note: 162

[167] "United Shoe Drops Suits" *Boston Herald* Boston, Massachusetts January 18, 1911, p. 12

[168] Engagement of Amy E. Plant Is Announced *Boston Journal* Boston, Massachusetts January 19, 1911, p. 4

[169] "Free To Draw On Account" *Springfield Daily News* Springfield, Massachusetts November 10, 1911, p.17

[170] Norfolk County, Massachusetts Registry of Deeds 1911-1912

[171] "Report Says Plants Have Healed Domestic Breach" *Boston Journal* Boston, Massachusetts June 3, 1912, p. 3

[172] "Plant And Wife Reconciled" *The Chicago Record-Herald* Chicago, Illinois June 1, 1912, p. 1

[173] "Mrs. Plant Declares She Is Not Reconciled To Husband" *Boston Sunday Post* Boston, Massachusetts June 16, 1912, p. 21

[174] Personal notes made in telephone conversation with John W. Dewey, Olive Dewey Plant's nephew November 29, 2012

[175] "Plant Divorce Will Be Tried" *Boston Herald* Boston, Massachusetts October 19, 1912, p. 5

[176] "Wife Of Thomas G. Plant Gets Divorce Decree After Hearing" *Boston Herald* Boston, Massachusetts October 29, 1912, p. 3

[177] List or Manifest of Alien Passengers in 1912, 1913 and 1922 give similar information regarding NYC address

[178] "Mrs. Plant Becomes New York Resident" *Boston Herald* Boston, Massachusetts November 14, 1912, p. 4

[179] Job Number 09196 Mrs. C. G. Plant Olmsted Research Guide Online

[180] "10 Homes That Matter" Randy Noles *Winter Park Magazine* Winter Park, Florida June 4, 2010

[181] "Mrs. Plant Leaves $150,000 to 'Poor' of Cohasset" *Boston Evening Globe* Boston, Massachusetts July 9, 1947, pp. 1. 2

[182] Town of Moultonboro, Collector's Sale of Real Estate, 1937 Book 212, page 501 (Thomas G. Plant 6,635 Acres) Carroll County (NH) Registry of Deeds

[183] Leander G. Pynn's Autobiographical Notes Castle in the Clouds Archives

[184] "A Man And His Mountains" E. L. D. Seymour *New Country Life Magazine* Doubleday Page & Company Garden City, New York February 1917

[185] List of Passengers on the S.S. Mauretania, Roll - T715, 1897-1957 1001-2000 1714 ancestry.com

[186] "Short Locals" *Stark County News* Toulon, Illinois December 4, 1912, p. 4

[187] *Dewey Family History* Dewey Publishing Company Westfield, Massachusetts 1898

[188] "Charles P. Dewey" *Stark County Illinois and Its People* Chicago, Illinois The Pioneer Publishing Company 1916

[189] "Daniel Dunham" *History of DuPage County, Illinois* Rufus Blanchard, O. L. Baskin & Co., Historical Publishers, 1882

[190] "Daniel Dunham" Obituary *Stark County News* Toulon, Illinois November 30, 1910, pp. 1, 8

[191]"Toulon Academy Commencement" *Stark County News* Toulon, Illinois April 26, 1901, p. 7

[192] Personal notes made by the late Penelope Hartshorne Batcheler, a retired National Park Service Historical Architect, in interviews with Tom Beal, J. Williams Beal's grandson, 2004

[193] "Architect Beal Dies in Hanover" *The Technology Review* 1919 Vol. 21 p. 576

[194] Information about John Williams Beal contained in a letter from his daughter-in-law, Mrs. John Woodbridge Beal written on her letterhead and signed Grace Beal, September 28, 1976

[195] ibid.

[196] Charles A. Burdett House "Broadview" Bartlett, New Hampshire Historical Society Judy Curtis and Eliza Jane Curtis, May 2011

[197] "Mollie (Mary Howe) Beal's Diary" Hanover Historical Society Hanover, Massachusetts

[198] "The Fireproof House" Jared Stuyvesant *House and Garden Magazine* McBride, Winston & Co. New York, New York January 1911 p. 13

[199] Barba + Wheelock, Architectural, Preservation + Design Firm in Portland, Maine survey begun in 2004

[200] The Aeolian Company Opus 1257 The Residence of Thomas G. Plant Moultonboro, New Hampshire March 31, 1913

[201] Notes made by Ann Hackl in telephone interviews with John Woodbridge Beal's two sons, Tom and Philip Beal February 6 and February 7, 2004

[202] Beal Family History compiled by Elizabeth Beal Kurzawski, granddaughter of John Woodbridge Beal

[203] Notes made by Ann Hackl in her telephone interview with Tom Beal, John Woodbridge Beal's son February 6, 2004

[204] See note: 197

[205] See note: 202

[206] Article in *Granite State News* Wolfeboro, NH March 18, 1911

[207] "T. G. Plant In $75,000 Suit" *Boston Herald* Boston, Massachusetts August 5, 1919, p. 3

[208] "T. G. Plant Estate Laborers Shoot Up Moultonboro" *Boston Herald* Boston, Massachusetts August 5, 1911, pages 1, 2

[209] See note: 207

[210] "Court Record And Calendar" *Boston Herald* Boston, Massachusetts February 3, 1922 p. 23

[211] "Spite Fence For Neighbors" *New York Times* New York, New York February 26, 1912, p. 7

[212] "Novel Spite Fence on Ossipee Mountain" *The Boston Sunday Globe* Boston, Massachusetts February 25, 1912, p. 16

[213] "Plant's Purpose" Thomas G. Plant Interview by George F. Bacon *Granite State News* January 13, 1912

[214] Excerpt from Leander Pynn's autobiography. Packard #20644 model 30 - Tim Martin, Packard Registry

[215] ibid.

[216] "Plant To Take Smith Award to Supreme Court" *Boston Journal* Boston, Massachusetts May 3, 1912, p. 11

[217] James A. Hutchinson v. Thomas G. Plant 218 Mass. 148

[218] See note: 188

[219] "Central Leather Shows Gains" *The Wall Street Journal* New York, New York March 27, 1917 p. 4 "As To Hides and Leather" *New York Times* New York, New York, April 15, 1917 p. 30

[220] Judith Dewey Newell, Olive's niece identified the Plant's travels to include Bermuda 1914-15, Hawaiian Islands 1915-16, Nassau 1916-17, Cuba 1917, Florida 1917, Canadian Rockies (undated) and Yosemite 1920 - information taken from an album. She believes they traveled to India.

[221] *This Day In Cuban History* Pedro Roig, Executive Director of the Cuban Studies Institute November 1, 2018

[222] Thomas Gustave Plant, Probate Records, Carroll County Court House, Ossipee, New Hampshire

[223] "United Shoe Co. Wins Supreme Court Case" *Boston Herald* Boston, Massachusetts February 4, 1913 pp. 1, 8

[224] "Decision in Plant Suit" *Wall Street Journal* New York, New York November 3, 1913, p. 5

[225] State of New Jersey Vital Records Abstract Certification April 20, 2013

226 "Record of Marriages Vol VI, p. 264" Marie Mahler, Historian for the Midvale United Methodist Church, Wanaque, New Jersey Tom and Olive Plants marriage May 3, 1912

227 Skyline Sketches "Lucknow: Castle in the Clouds" by Stan and Maryjane Bean *Appalachia AMC* Boston, Massachusetts June 1974 pp. 151—155

228 "Short Locals" *Stark County News* Toulon, Illinois December 31, 1913 p. 10

229 Dr. Robert Newton, Professor Emeritus, Geosciences, Smith College; Northampton, Massachusetts

230"Masonry Survey" Richard Irons, Restoration Mason Limerick, Maine Site Visit. May 26, 2005

231 Author's Conversations with Steve Swenson, former owner of Redstone Quarry in Conway, New Hampshire February 2021

232 See note: 230

233 "Mr. and Mrs. Fred Larrabee Feted On 60th Anniversary At W. Bath" *Portland Press Herald* Portland, Maine January 31, 1950 p. 6

234 "Mr. and Mrs. Fred W. Larrabee of West Bath Married 50 Years" *Bath Independent* Bath, Maine February 1, 1940 pp. 1, 6

235 ibid.

236 See note: 192 Penelope Hartshorne Batcheler

237 "Lucknow, National Register of Historic Places Nomination" Elizabeth Durfee Hengen, Preservation Consultant and Peter Michaud, New Hampshire Division of Historical Resources March 2018

238 "Stockton Springs" *The Republican Journal* Belfast, Maine August 7, 1913 p. 4

239 Lord & Burnham Archives, The LuEsther T. Mertz Library, The New York Botanical Garden; Bronx, New York. 10438-5126

240 "Takes Ohio Territory" *Boot and Shoe Recorder* Boston, Massachusetts February 2, 1918

241 " A. C. Grover Dies" *Boot and Shoe Recorder* Boston, Massachusetts August 29, 1920 p. 64

242 "Running A National Retail Shop Through Advertising" Lynn G. Wright *Printers' Ink, A Journal For Advertisers, Vol. LXXI*. New York, New York June 2, 1910. Pp. 34-36

243 "Portraits By A, Jongers" *New York Times* New York, New York December 23, 1906 p. 10

244 Personal notes made in telephone conversation with Phelps Dewey, Olive Plant's nephew August 2, 2013

[245] "Uncle Sam To Publish Business Newspaper" *Indianapolis Star* Indianapolis, Indiana January 2, 1915 p. 2

[246]"Judgment For Thomas G. Plant" *Boston Evening Transcript* Boston, Massachusetts January 29, 1915 p. 5

[247] "Lake Association Elects" *Boston Globe* Boston, Massachusetts August 1, 1915 p. 9

[248] "Prize Sheep And Collies Arrive For Plant Farm" *Boston Herald* Boston, Massachusetts June 28, 1916 p. 2

[249] "Newfoundland Man's Promotion" *The St. John's Daily Star* St. John, Newfoundland January 11, 1917 p. 8

[250] See Note: 220 Judith Dewey Newell

[251] Wellesley College Class Notes, Class of 1905 Olive Dewey (Mrs. Thomas G. Plant) 1930 Wellesley College Archives Wellesley, Massachusetts

[252] "Drives To The Top of Ossipee Mountain" 21 page brochure and map 1916

[253] "Thomas G. Plant's Good Example" *Boston Herald* Boston, Massachusetts November 20, 1916 p. 10

[254] "Ossipee Mountain Park, a Paradise of Woodlands and Water Falls" *Boston Sunday Herald* Boston, Massachusetts September 30, 1917 Section E, page 6

[255] "Maine Gossip" *Daily Kennebec Journal* Kennebec, Maine November 2, 1916 p. 6

[256] "Bath's Beautiful And Homelike Old Folks Home" *Bath Daily Times* Bath, Maine November 10, 1917 p. 1

[257] "Old Folks Home" *The Bath Independent"* Bath, Maine November 4, 1916 p. 7

[258] "First Bill Passed By House Was Sagadahoc Measure" *The Bath Independent* Bath, Maine February 10, 1917 p. 11

[259] "Bath, Municipal Campaign Will Be Short and Active" *Boston Sunday Globe* Boston, Massachusetts February 25, 1917

[260] "Old Folks Home Folks Have Tree" *Bath Independent* Bath, Maine December 28, 1918 p. 6

[261] "Ford Buys Steam Yacht" *The Sun* New York, New York February 1, 1917 p. 15

[262] "Lucknow, A Mountain and Lake Estate" *Country Life* Advertisement Doubleday, Page & Company Garden City, New York. October 1924

[263] "Plant Building Finest Links In Whole Country" *Bath Independent* Bath, Maine August 7, 1919 p. 2

[264] *The Castle and the Club, The Bald Peak Colony Club* Elizabeth Crawford Wilkin Melvin Village, New Hampshire 1964 pp. 12-13

[265] ibid. p.17

[266] "New Hampshire Good Roads Delegates Named" *Boston Sunday Globe* Boston, Massachusetts April 4, 1920 p. 14

[267] "Somersworth" *Boston Globe* Boston, Massachusetts January 22, 1922 p. 18

[268] "British Golfers Lose Exhibition" *Boston Globe* Boston, Massachusetts August 6, 1922 p. 15

[269] "P. D. Haughton Buys Boston Nationals" *New York Times* New York, New York January 9, 1916 pp. 48, 50

[270] "The Castle and the Club, The Bald Peak Colony Club" Elizabeth Crawford Wilkin Melvin Village, New Hampshire 1964 p. 25

[271] *Pinehurst Outlook* Pinehurst, North Carolina December 22, 1921 p. 1

[272] *The Castle and the Club, The Bald Peak Colony Club* Elizabeth Crawford Wilkin Melvin Village, New Hampshire 1964 Mrs. Wilkin's review of the Club minutes

[273] Guy Davison, Meredith Ford ...Leander Pynn's autobiography undated

[274] "Old Folks Home Donor Visits The Institution" *Bath Independent* Bath, Maine. November 15, 1933 p. 2

[275] New Hampshire, U. S. Death Record 2002 1934, April 18 William Franklin Plant

[276] Carroll County Registry of Deeds Ossipee, NH Carroll County Book 210, p. 198

[277] Carroll County Registry of Deeds Ossipee, NH Carroll County Book 206, p. 341

[278] Carroll County Registry of Deeds Ossipee, NH Carroll County Book 215, p. 518

[279]" Petition #11,951 Estate of Joseph H. Emery by Caroline Griggs Plant of Winter Park, Florida May 25, 1942

[280] Carroll County Registry of Deeds Ossipee, NH Carroll County Book 217, p. 10

[281] "Lucknow, A Mountain Estate in Moultonborough, New Hampshire" a website maintained by Ron Tobey, the grandson of the second owner of the estate.

[282] Carroll County Registry of Deeds Ossipee, NH Carroll County Book 220, p. 306

[283] Author's Personal Telephone calls with John W. Dewey, Phelps Dewey and Judith Dewey Newell

[284] "Thomas G. Plant Dead" *The Wyoming Post Herald* Wyoming, Illinois July 30, 1941 p. 8

[285] "Hold Funeral Rites Monday, C. P. Dewey, 86" *Stark County News* Toulon, Illinois October 20, 1943 pp. 1, 8